TOW TRUCK KINGS 2

MORE Secrets of the Towing & Recovery Business

ALLAN T. DUFFIN

published by

duffin creative

los angeles

Table of Contents

Introduction   ix

MEETING THE PEOPLE

My Funniest Incident   1

A Family of Pioneers: An Exclusive Interview   7
with Jerry Holmes

Charity Towers   13

Pamela Oakes: Car Care Crusader   19

Incident Management and the I-95   25
Corridor Coalition:
An Interview with Capt. Tom Martin

Photographing the World's Greatest   31
Tow Trucks: The Life Journey of Earl Johnson

'Tis the Season for Towers: 37
Gift-Giving for the Holidays

Tornado Watch: Towers Engage   43
in Disaster Relief Efforts

BREAKING THE BANK

Getting the Dough to Keep the Shop Running: 51
Finance in a Time of Distress

Collections: Getting What's Owed   57

Processing Credit Cards for Your Towing   65
Business

TOW TRUCKS
AND OTHER EQUIPMENT

Equipment Improvements for Better   73
Towing

Voice of the Customer: 79
Improving Towing Equipment

Chassis: Targeting the One You Want   85

Can You Find Me Now? Tracking   91
Your Tow Trucks

Parts: The Popular, the Most Useful,   99
and the Ones You Should Know About

BETTER BUSINESS FOR EVERYONE

The Truth About Overtime   107

Education and Training   113
for Tow Truck Drivers

Computer Solutions in the Shop   123
and on the Road

Best Defense: Legal Protection   129
in the Shop and on the Road

Working Smarter, Leading More Effectively: 135
Better Business Management for the Tower

GETTING INTO THE CLUB

Repossession: A Tough Job   145
for the Right Tower

Motor Clubs: Towing Partners   155

Towing Associations: Bringing Everyone   161
(and Everything) Together

**WHAT YOU SEE IS WHAT YOU
(MIGHT) GET**

Signage: Keeping it Effective and Legal   171

Get the Word Out: Advertising Tricks   177
and Tips for Towers

Safety and Signals: Protecting Your Customers   185

Introduction

As a freelance writer, I've covered a lot of different subjects. This collection of stories was selected from my work as a regular contributor to *Towing & Recovery Footnotes,* the newspaper of the towing industry, which publishes print and digital editions.

Tow Truck Kings 2 features stories, tips, tricks, and information that makes for great reading for people already in the business, or as a primer or textbook for anyone interested in the industry. I've included chapters about legends of the industry, towing efforts following natural disasters, bill collecting and credit card processing, working with customers, GPS tracking, overtime, effective use of computers in a business setting, legal issues, repossession efforts, motor clubs, towing associations, and advertising, plus humorous stories from the road.

I hope you enjoy the book. If you have any questions, please feel free to contact me through my website at www.aduffin.com.

—Allan T. Duffin

My Funniest Incident

A dog and a hearse

We got a call from a customer who got stuck in a snow bank. Upon pulling up on the scene, to our surprise, we found out that the vehicle in the ditch was a hearse. It had plowed through the snow bank and was good and stuck. (The back of the hearse was empty — no coffin inside.)

We hooked on and started winching. We had to use the hydraulics of the truck instead of the winch, as the weight of the car was just too much on the winch.

After about 20 minutes we got the hearse out of the snow. Amazingly the vehicle only had minor cosmetic damage — a piece of chrome and some plastics were broken. The snow was so packed into the wheel wells that the wheels would only turn to the right. Once we dug the snow out from around the wheel wells, the hearse was drivable again.

The customer followed us back to the shop to pay the bill, then explained what had happened: His dog — a 150-pound bull mastiff named Guido! — had leapt from the back of the hearse into the front seat. The dog climbed into the driver's lap and pinned him against the door of the car. The driver lost control of the car, which then flew into the ditch. Fortunately neither the driver nor the dog was injured.

— *Brian, Matt and Ryan Totman, Totman Enterprises, Inc., Searsmont, Maine*

Not on fire

I went to do a tow that was a hundred miles away from home in a snowstorm. It was around 3 a.m. I was in my brand new International truck with a car carrier deck on it.

I finally got on scene and loaded the vehicle up. When we all got in the truck the passenger closed the door — and somehow set off the fire extinguisher!

After about 20 minutes we got the hearse out of the snow. Amazingly the vehicle only had minor cosmetic damage — a piece of chrome and some plastics were broken. The snow was so packed into the wheel wells that the wheels would only turn to the right. Once we dug the snow out from around the wheel wells, the hearse was drivable again.

There we were, a hundred miles from home, inside a cab full of yellow fire retardant substance. The inside of the cab was yellow, I was yellow and the customer was yellow. I can still taste that stuff and boy, was it hard to clean out. Moral of the story: never place a fire extinguisher where a customer or a door can set it off!

— *Chuck Ceccarelli, Idaho Wrecker Sales, Mountain Home, Idaho*

Starting the car

The other day I towed a car approximately 15 miles across town to the local Toyota dealer for a no-start problem. Per the dealership's instructions we don't attempt to start vehicles, so we wheel-lifted the vehicle and towed it in.

We hooked on and started winching. We had to use the hydraulics of the truck instead of the winch, as the weight of the car was just too much on the winch.

After we reached the dealership the service writer greeted us at the door and started his paperwork. When I handed him the keys he noticed there was a solid steel key for a Toyota, along with the factory computer key. The driver, a young man getting ready to graduate from college, had a lot on his mind and didn't realize that he was trying to use the steel key to start the car — you have to use the factory computer chip key instead.

We used the computer key, and the car started right up while still on the tow truck.

While it wasn't too funny, I'll always remember the look of awe on the customer's face. He paid his bill, having enjoyed a ride across town in a tow truck.

— *Nick Schade, Tony's Wrecker Service, Inc., Louisville, Ky.*

Thanks, Dad

Several years ago at the Ohio tow show, Bill and Marcie Gratzianna from the TV series "Wrecked: Life in the Crash Lane" showed up and were signing autographs. I watched this little boy standing in line. When he reached the front, Bill talked to him. The little boy stuttered, "I — I — I know you!" Bill said, "That nice," shook the boy's hand and signed a poster for him.

That little boy turned around, looked at his dad and said, "I'm glad you're a tower."

After about 20 minutes we got the hearse out of the snow. Amazingly the vehicle only had minor cosmetic damage — a piece of chrome and some plastics were broken. The snow was so packed into the wheel wells that the wheels would only turn to the right. Once we dug the snow out from around the wheel wells, the hearse was drivable again.

That's a moment that will live with me for the rest of my life, because that little boy was the proudest kid in the world.

— *Don Mesaros, Auto Works Heavy, Milford, Ohio*

Lost and found

During the winter of 1996, I was towing a VW bug for the police department. I'd put the VW on a wheel lift truck and was headed back to my lot at 3 a.m. I was in a hurry and failed to properly secure both wheels

3

to the wheel lift. Along my route — and unknown to me! — the car came off the wheel lift completely, at the bottom of a steep hill.

I drove the remaining two miles to my lot, exited the truck, opened the gate and pulled into the lot. I then looked in my mirror to back the VW into a spot when I noticed the car was gone! The wheel lift, straps — all were in place. "Oh my gosh!" I thought. I quickly drove the same route back, looking for the car to be wrecked or sitting somewhere in the road.

I arrived back at the exact place I had hooked up the car. The police officer was still there. He remarked that I was quick and that there was nothing else to tow off. I did not want to say anything about the missing car.

I immediately began driving the same route over and over again, looking everywhere for the car. I thought, "Maybe it came off and someone stole it? Maybe the car ran off the road and is hidden somewhere in the darkness?" I drove slower and slower, still hunting for this light blue VW bug.

As the sun was coming up, I noticed some tire tracks in the morning dew in a grassy downhill slope. I followed the tracks, running on foot.

The tracks ended at the front door of an old barn. I opened the doors to the barn — and there sat the VW, with its nose up against bales of hay. The VW had hit the barn doors perfectly in the middle and the doors swung open. The VW had rolled inside, and the barn doors closed behind it.

I propped open the barn doors, started the VW and drove it back to my truck. Then I towed it back to the lot. No damage! After weeks of the VW being stored in my lot, the owner finally came to get his vehicle. He complained that the front bumper had straw sticking out of it. I gladly removed the straw and had to keep from laughing as I released the car to him.

I never told anyone about this until 10 years later. Now it's my funny story after 31 years in the towing business!

— *Mike Patellis, Alpha Towing, Inc., Marietta, Ga.*

Four-legged recovery

The funniest recovery I've ever done was recovering a horse out of a creek. The horse had broken out of the stables, ran into a creek, and got tangled up in some branches that were lying loose in the water.

The owner of the horse called and asked us if we could recover his horse out of the creek. I'm thinking, "Well, that's a new one on me, but sure, we'll do anything."

I went out myself. We strapped up underneath the horse, and actually lifted the horse up on straps, over the creek.

I tell people that story every now and then, and they tell me, "There's no way you could get a horse out of a creek!"

— *Louis Anglin, General Automotive Services, Searcy, Ark.*

A Family of Pioneers:
An Exclusive Interview with Jerry Holmes

Many people in the towing industry own, or work for, towing companies that are family operated. But what about the granddaddy of all family tow truck firms, the Holmes Company?

Gerald (Jerry) Holmes, grandson of the company's founder and a pioneer in his own right, has some great stories about his family's role in the towing and recovery industry; the creation of his own firm, the Century Wrecker Company; and what he's doing today.

The story of the American tow truck industry began almost a century ago — with a seat-of-the-pants contraption that launched a family dynasty.

An engineer's journey

In 1916, Ernest Holmes, Sr., an auto mechanic in Chattanooga, Tenn., rescued a Model T car after the driver accidentally ran it off the road.

Holmes finagled a makeshift towing assembly with a pulley, a chain and three poles. After pulling the Model T out of the water, Holmes realized that he was on to something: why not take his ideas about towing and turn them into a business? He gathered his ideas together, opened a small facility and began manufacturing tow trucks and towing equipment.

As it grew, the Holmes Company remained a family operation. Ernest Holmes, Jr., became president after his father died in the early 1940s. His son Jerry grew up surrounded by towing technology, and hoped from an early age that he would someday join the family business.

"I was never promised, but I hoped and prepared for it," said Holmes. "I was always interested in mechanical things. My brothers always accused me of tearing their toys apart and never putting them back together!"

While studying engineering at Georgia Tech — his father's alma mater — Holmes spent his summers working at the family's company. He became a full-time employee in the summer of 1954, immediately after graduating from college. He would stay for nearly two decades.

Although he was a third-generation member of the family, Holmes was given no freebies. He had to work his way up the ladder just like everyone else, beginning his career in an entry-level position. "I started as a draftsman, on a drawing board," recalled Holmes. "Then I became a designer, still on a drawing board."

When the company's chief engineer passed away, Holmes filled the suddenly empty desk and eventually rose to the position of vice president of engineering. "In that job I was responsible for product design as well as plant engineering," explained Holmes.

In 1972, after more than 50 years in the business, Ernest Holmes, Jr., decided to retire, and the Holmes family sold the company that bore its name. The Dover Corporation, an industrial manufacturer with a history of acquiring manufacturing firms, purchased the Holmes Company.

Though he decided to stay and work for the new hierarchy, Holmes eventually realized that it was time for him to strike out on his own. "The Dover Corporation came in with their own ideas in mind, and began to create changes that I wasn't happy with," said Holmes. "One thing I remember was that I had product ideas that weren't readily accepted by management."

One of those ideas was the creation of hydraulically operated towing equipment. But at the time, said Holmes, "They weren't ready for hydraulics." Holmes remained with Dover for a year and a half, then announced that he was leaving.

In 1974 Holmes and his youngest brother, Bill, founded Century Wrecker Company in nearby Ooltewah, Tenn. There they could fully explore their new engineering ideas, including the use of hydraulics — a concept that would transform the towing and recovery industry.

Technological milestones

During his lengthy career, Holmes was a witness to — and a participant in — many milestones in towing technology. Public and government concern over automobile safety in the 1950s and 1960s led to massive changes in vehicle design. The towing industry had to modify its on-scene methods accordingly. "There was an increased concern for safety in towing, and eliminating damage to the towed vehicle," explained Holmes. "We needed better damage control."

The safety revolution sparked a new spirit of cooperation between the Holmes Company and major automobile manufacturers. "We were able to get preliminary viewings of the prototypes to see what difficulties we might have in trying to tow these vehicles damage-free," recalled Holmes," and also what kinds of devices we could develop that would minimize damage."

"So we became involved with the automotive engineering departments of, at the very least, Chrysler, Ford and General Motors," continued Holmes. "At that time automobiles were being designed without bumpers as we know them today, and all these fiberglass spoilers that hung down were subject to a lot of damage. Early on, the car designers were not thinking about what could happen to these delicate underbody parts."

Not satisfied with the old hook-and-chain method — and aware of the scratching and damage that it could cause to the towed vehicle — the Holmes Company introduced and patented the towing sling.

During that period, Holmes also recalls a crucial change in the business side of the house: "There was a drift in the industry away from service stations — who were performing the vast majority of the towing, at least where smaller vehicles were concerned — and toward professional towing operators. I thought this was a good move," he said.

In the mid-1970s towing technology took another giant leap forward as hydraulics became standard equipment. Century Wrecker Company — the firm that Holmes founded — was at the forefront of this progress. As the next decade began, Century developed a practical hydraulic wheel lift system for cars. This led to super-duty underlift systems for trucks and buses as well.

Holmes is understandably proud of the truck chassis and equipment that he helped design and build. "Holmes and Century had a great reputation for quality and innovation," said Holmes, "and were always leaders in the industry. It seemed like most of our competition kind of tried to follow what we did after the fact — not all of them, but it seems like most of them did."

Today, Miller Industries owns the Holmes and Century brands and carries on both nameplates' proud traditions, manufacturing new equipment at the Miller factory in Ooltewah, near Chattanooga, and at other locations.

Words of wisdom

What advice does Holmes have for people who want to start their own towing company? "You need hands-on experience," he said, "maybe five years of actual grunt work — getting under there and hooking them up and doing the driving. Don't start [a business] until you know what you're doing."

When hanging your own shingle, Holmes recommends that new business owners start small. "Don't bet all of your assets on a startup if you can possibly avoid it," he said. "A lot of startups fail. You learn the hard way." If the business doesn't succeed, "it would be nice if you retain enough assets to do it again, or to try something else." In addition, said Holmes, company owners should keep their debt to a safe level.

Prior to launching the Century Wrecker Company, Holmes felt he was "weak in bookkeeping and financial management." So he went back to school and earned a master's degree in business administration. In addition, he said he was not afraid to seek help and to hire part-time

10

employees to help with the bookkeeping for his new company.

Finally, said Holmes, "When we started Century we set a five-year goal. You have to set reasonable goals and then try to obtain them."

Time at home

Eventually Holmes decided he'd had a good run in the industry and decided to retire. Today he enjoys boating and powerboating. "The principal social activity for us is the Chattanooga Yacht Club, which I've belonged to since 1971," said Holmes.

A supportive spouse can make all the difference in the world, and Holmes' wife Betsye has encouraged his efforts over the years. When they met, Betsye was a beautician in Chattanooga, where they still live today. "She owned her own shop and had a very great following here," recalled Holmes.

"Betsye and I were introduced as she came out of a local restaurant some 50 years ago," Holmes continued. "I was blown away. She was beautiful and still is." Over the years, added Holmes, "[Betsye] has been nothing but supportive, and always involved and always interested in what we're doing," said Holmes.

Holmes has always had an interest in flying. A veteran of the U.S. Air Force, he earned his private pilot's license when he was just 17 years old. "Shortly after that I got involved in college and getting married and all that goes with it," he recalled," so I didn't resume flying until I retired from Century." In short order, Holmes got his instrument, multi-engine and seaplane ratings, and flew small aircraft from the Chattanooga airport until about five years ago, when he decided he was a little long in the tooth for the sport and decided to focus on other pursuits instead.

You might be surprised to learn that this veteran tower also likes railroads — but on a much smaller scale. Ten years ago Holmes built an addition to his house so that he could create a model railroad layout. It's an ongoing project, as he adds new features all the time. "I've always wanted to build a lifelike model railroad," said Holmes. "It'll never be finished," he chuckled, "but it keeps me out of trouble."

Finally and most important, Holmes and his wife enjoy spending time with their children and grandchildren, all of whom live in Texas.

"We make two or three trips out there a year to visit them," said Holmes. It's all part of a life well lived by an innovator in a family of innovators, a pioneer in an industry that continues to utilize and refine the products that he and his family introduced over the years.

Charity Towers

During the holiday season, towers get into the spirit of giving — not only for their families and friends, but also for charitable organizations in their communities. Whether a towing company is a single shop or a large network, there are many ways that towers help make lives better for people in need. From small raffles to huge parades, towers sponsor and participate in a wide variety of charity events.

Being sporty

In Athens, Tenn., Jerry's Garage & Wrecker Service uses one of its trucks and a man-lift to hang advertising banners for the annual Shriner's Rodeo. "We provide free towing if it rains and vehicles get stuck," said owner Jerry Riggs, "along with free boost-offs if they leave their lights on by mistake, or something along those lines." After the rodeo is over, Jerry's Towing removes the banners.

Speed's Towing in Portland, Ore., sponsors an annual charity golf tournament. "This year we raised $5,000 and donated it to the Make-A-Wish Foundation," said Gary Coe, the owner of Speed's Towing. For the

13

past 30 years Make-A-Wish has helped children with life-threatening medical conditions, granting those kids the ability to fulfill the dream of a lifetime.

Coe said that Speed's Towing works with a different charity during each golf tournament. A recent event generated $4,000, which Speed's donated to the Oregon Humane Society. The Humane Society recently opened a new 24-hour medical care facility for the 10,000 animals that arrive in its care every year.

On parade

Imagine several hundred tow trucks, bumper-to-bumper, driving together for charity. If you've participated in the annual Tow Trucks for Tots parade, then you know just how amazing this lineup of vehicles looks as it traverses the Midwest.

Pat Winer, owner of Worldwide Equipment Sales in Rockdale, Ill., sponsored the first Tow Trucks for Tots parade in November 2008. Two hundred thirty-nine tow trucks traveled a 40-mile route from Joliet to Bridgeview, landing the parade in the Guinness Book of World Records as the longest parade of tow trucks in history.

Winer wanted to contribute to the community but was looking for a unique way in which to do it. "I wanted to help less fortunate children who couldn't enjoy a Christmas morning full of toys," explained Winer, who hit on the idea of sponsoring a parade as the centerpiece of a local charity drive. Participants could donate toys at any of 50 drop-off locations — including Winer's office and many towing companies — in the Chicago metropolitan area.

Word about the event spread quickly. "Towing companies find out about the parade through our Web site, by word of mouth, and articles in various publications," said Winer.

This year's Tow Trucks for Tots parade, held on November 8, featured vehicles from more than 190 towing companies. The parade started at the Caterpillar plant in Rockdale at 9:00 a.m. Participants drove their tow trucks 41 miles to the Toyota Park stadium in Bridgeview.

The parade organizers encourage the public to participate as well. "We ask that they line the parade route," explained Winer, "and at the end of the parade they come to Toyota Park to view the trucks up close."

Coincidentally, everything that's collected for the tow truck parade is given to another local organization — one that sponsors a parade of its own. "All toys and monetary donations are donated to the Chicagoland Toys for Tots Motorcycle Parade," said Winer. He's already busy planning his next tow truck parade.

Vehicle auctions

Another popular charity effort for towers is the vehicle auction. Since towers are used to working with vehicles, why not use that expertise to raise money for charity?

The ongoing auto auction at Speed's Towing in Portland generates $35,000 a week for local charities. "Over the years we've accumulated 22 different charities and non-profit organizations," explained Coe, "and have assisted them with, or initiated, their auto donation programs."

These charities include the American Council of the Blind, Father Joe's Villages, Goodwill, Northwest Children's Theatre and School, Paralyzed Veterans of America, Oregon Public Broadcasting, Portland Rescue Mission and the Father's Heart Street Ministry.

According to Coe, each charity or non-profit has a specific constituency to which it markets, and asks that constituency to donate cars and sometimes boats or recreational vehicles. "Then," said Coe, "we go pick up the vehicle, clean it up, test drive it if possible — we're located on a private road — and then sell it at the next weekly auction."

How did Coe get involved with vehicle auctions? The event had its beginnings in lien sales of cars from police and private impound tows. "My friends in San Diego at RoadOne West operate a very successful auction," explained Coe. "I went to school on how they operated their auction and who their charities were."

The auction is well-attended by a variety of clientele including auto dismantlers, used cars dealers, curb stoners (non-licensed dealers), "and lots of retail public," said Coe, adding that the event has become the largest public auction in the Portland area.

15

Showtime

A variation on this theme is the charity car and motorcycle show. A-Express Towing & Recovery of Palatine, Ill., sponsors this type of event at Melas Park in the nearby city of Mt. Prospect. Held in conjunction with the annual festival of the Mount Prospect Lions Club, the Lion's Paw Charity Car Show and Motorcycle Show runs over the Fourth of July holiday. For a $15 donation, vehicle owners get to show off their pride and joy.

A-Express sponsors the event with all proceeds going to the Lion's Paw Charity. According to Rob Habel, owner of A-Express, a recent event netted $2,400 from registration fees and raffles. Eighty-five participants displayed their cars to the public.

"The Lions Club's main focus as a charity is helping the sight- and hearing-impaired," said Habel. "They also help with natural disaster response. It's the largest service organization in the world."

Habel got involved in the car show four years ago, when the poor economy forced the original sponsor, a local auto dealer, to eliminate the event from its annual budget. "Originally we were just going to be a sponsor, but we ended up running it instead," said Habel. "My staff volunteers their time to the show. They help with contacting local businesses about raffle donations, and on the day of the show help with registration, setup of the cars, cleanup and distributing the raffles."

Habel's company pays all expenses associated with the show including trophies, magnetic dash plaques, and a DJ for music and entertainment. The raffle prizes are donated by local businesses and consist of anything from pens, hats and t-shirts to $125 certificates for car detailing. This year several outside vendors set up booths with products of interest to the car enthusiast.

From a business perspective, Habel noted that the car show is a great way for local businesses to network while helping their community. "Entry bags are given out to each participant," explained Habel. The bag contain items such as pens, paper, coupons for oil changes and advertising for local businesses.

Airborne tower

So far we've talked about ground-based charity efforts. But Ken Ulmer, president of Safetow in Houston, Texas, takes a different approach: he likes to deliver charity items by air. Ulmer, who also serves as the education chairman of the Texas Towing and Storage Association, uses his private plane to play Santa Claus as well as assisting with disaster relief.

Recently Ulmer and nine other pilots delivered Christmas gifts to underprivileged children in Galveston. "We loaded up our planes and flew down, just like Santa," said Ulmer. "Many of the kids were victims of the area ravaged by Hurricane Katrina."

Though he's unable to perform as much charity work as he'd like to, Ulmer is glad that he's been able to turn a hobby into something that can help his community. "I've wanted to be a pilot ever since I was seven years old," explained Ulmer, "and it finally became a reality in 2006." Ulmer's plane is a 2000 Piper Archer III, a four-seat single-engine model — perfect for delivering gifts or transporting passengers needing assistance.

Companies that care

Major companies that support the towing and recovery industry are hard at work improving things in their communities as well.

Smaller firms can sometimes pack just as much of a punch as the majors do. People who are familiar with the Landoll Corporation of Marysville, Kan., know that the company manufactures lowboy trailers that are popular with many towers. What you might not know, however, is that Landoll has a long history of supporting its community through charity efforts of all kinds. The 600-employee company regularly supports organizations like the Special Olympics, the ALS Foundation, Relay for Life, and schools and senior housing in its community.

Recently the company supplied labor, money, and spearheaded fundraising efforts to renovate St. Gregory's Elementary School. The $2.6 million project included the addition of a new parking lot and playground. In addition, Landoll renovated facilities at the local airport by supplying a portion of the funding, materials and all of the labor for the project.

The family-owned company is heavily involved in supporting nearby cities as well. Don Landoll (founder and CEO) and his brother Rich (the plant manager) provide "Angel Flights" to people in their community. Angel Flight is a nonprofit organization of volunteer pilots who transport residents in need of medical assistance to hospitals in major metropolitan areas such as Phoenix, Houston, Minneapolis, and Charlotte, N.C.

Another way that Landoll supports the community is by sharing its expertise with local residents. For many years, Don Landoll has hosted groups of students on tours through the Landoll facility. "He has given classroom presentations at Benedictine College and at one time taught an entrepreneurial class at Kansas State University," said Landoll-Smith. "We've been a long-time participant with the local high school's educational work programs including Future Farmers of America and the Family Career and Community Leaders of America."

Landoll-Smith also noted that the company strives to hire a diverse employee workforce. Landoll Corporation has partnered with Twin Valley Developmental Services for over a decade to employ several developmentally disabled workers.

All of these outreach efforts have been critical in maintaining a vibrant business for 46 years, said Landoll-Smith. "Landoll feels that it is the right thing to do — support those who support us," she explained. In fact, Landoll recently received the Kansas Governor's Award of Excellence for its support of the local community.

In the end, it's not just about the tow. By using whatever resources they have, charitable towers make a difference in their communities each and every day of the year.

Pamela Oakes: Car Care Crusader

Pam Oakes may live and work in sunny climes but her roots are far north, in the Motor City — Detroit, Michigan. A fourth-generation maintenance technician, Oakes owns Pam's Motor City Automotive, which serves southwest Florida and is the area's largest vehicle repair facility.

Oakes grew up in the automotive industry. "My great-grandfather, Leonard Smith, started out with Huppmobile in the mid-1920s," said Oakes. (Huppmobile produced cars during the first half of the 20th Century, a time when the "Big Three" automakers — Chrysler, Ford and General Motors — gradually came to dominate a marketplace that previously hosted many other automobile manufacturers.)

Smith was originally a police officer with the Detroit Police Department, but his wife convinced him to switch careers into something safer. It was the time of Prohibition in America, and bootleggers moving illegal goods through the Great Lakes sometimes resorted to violence to get their products where they were supposed to go.

Smith opened his own garage in the late 1920s. Although it was a safer place than the police department, he nevertheless came face-to-face with gangsters in his new line of work. "My great-grandfather — though not by choice — worked on vehicles owned by the Purple Gang and other minor bootleggers who ran liquor from Canada to Chicago," explained Oakes.

"My grandfather really didn't have a choice but to work on the bootleggers' vehicles," added Oakes. "He would tell us that they would come into the shop, unsolicited. He would fix their vehicles while they played cards and drank (liquor). He said that he didn't hold conversations or make small talk. He didn't want any trouble for himself or family members. It was a very violent time in places like Detroit, Chicago, and the like, and he did not want to introduce that into his family life."

At the beginning of World War II Smith decided to help with the war effort. He closed his shop and got a job at the Dodge Main plant in Detroit, where he remained for the rest of his career. Later, his son — Oakes' grandfather — joined Dodge and worked at the same factory. Then *his* son, Jerry — Pam Oakes' father — entered the automotive industry as well, working as an independent technician on the east side of Detroit. "He specialized in steering gear and suspension," said Oakes.

Pam Oakes' interest in cars began in the late 1960s when she was just a little girl. "My dad and great-grandfather would always let me watch while they worked on their own vehicles," said Oakes. "I remember climbing up on the fender of my great-grandfather's 1969 Plymouth (which I still have to this day) while he showed me how to set a choke on a carburetor." It was Oakes' first lesson in vehicle maintenance, and she loved it.

"My great-grandparents and parents were very big in my life," Oakes recalled fondly. "They were always telling me to 'watch this' or say, 'Look how I am doing this.' And that's how I learned the basics."

Oakes went to college, majoring in English, EET (Electronic Engineering Technology) and general studies. She worked her way through college as a reporter, and upon graduation launched a career as a newspaper reporter and editor. However, she still kept a hand in the auto industry, repairing and showing classic and antique cars in her spare time.

After 11 years in the newspaper industry, Oakes decided it was time for a career change. She contacted her father, who was working at an independent garage in Fort Myers, Fla. "I called him and asked him to make room for me," said Oakes. "That was 18 years ago!"

Going independent

Oakes worked at that garage for about one and a half years. She wasn't thrilled with the environment there and wanted to make a change. "I thought, 'Hey, I could do this better,'" recalled Oakes. "I didn't like that they treated everyone as a number and not as a person with a problem car."

In 1995, Oakes opened the doors to her own business. True to her background as a Detroit native, she named the company Pam's Motor City Automotive. In the beginning, her business had one employee: Oakes herself. "I was the technician, service writer, bookkeeper, et cetera," she said.

One month later, Oakes added a lube tech. Within a year she was able to hire a second technician, and later her father joined her as the company's tire manager and tire tech. In 2002 — seven years after she started the business — Oakes hired a contractor to build a 12-bay shop. At the time Oakes had 15 employees working under her roof.

Over the years the shop continued to be a family operation: Oakes' mother came on staff as the company bookkeeper. (She recently retired from the position.)

Four generations of good advice

When her customers ask her for advice about performing their own repairs, Oakes warns them that cars and trucks can be complicated and advises against do-it-yourself repairs. Instead, Oakes stresses the importance of preventative maintenance — knowing how to maintain, rather than repair, a vehicle.

Giving advice to customers came naturally for Oakes, and she decided to write about the topic as well. In 1996 she delved into her experience as a journalist and began penning articles and books about consumer car care.

21

Oakes also got into video production, creating a car care program for her Spanish-speaking customers. She wrote the videos with one of her long-time employees, and was recognized by the Car Care Council Women's Board for her efforts.

Then it was time to put all of her expertise in one volume. To provide vehicle owners with a concise overview of preventative maintenance, Oakes wrote the book *Car Care for the Clueless (or How You Can 'Make Money' While Maintaining Your Vehicle).*

"This is not a 'how to fix it' manual but a consumer car care awareness book," Oakes explained. "The easy-to-read, non-technical jargon helps the consumer avoid the pitfalls of car care maintenance while making some money maintaining their vehicle."

In the book Oakes provides a variety of tips and tricks for vehicle owners, including advice such as not letting your gas tank go below a quarter full. "Your vehicle's fuel economy will diminish while it goes into a 'diagnostic mode,'" said Oakes.

In addition, said Oakes, vehicle owners should use a "top tier" fuel no matter what octane they prefer, in order to get optimum fuel economy and performance. "Top tier" gasoline contains higher levels of detergents than the standard versions, helping prevent engine buildup.

Elsewhere in *Car Care for the Clueless,* Oakes dispenses advice on topics including how to be a good customer (and how it will save money) and the benefits of not using nitrogen in your vehicle's tires. In addition, she said, "There is no such thing as a 'free' tire."

Charging ahead

Over the years Oakes has received much recognition in her community. For 13 years the *Ft. Myers News-Press* recognized her shop as providing the Best Auto Repair in southwest Florida. Pam's Motor City Automotive has been honored in industry magazines such as *Motorage, Tire Review,* and even *Parent & Child* and *Senior Life.* (Oakes wrote a "senior edition" of *Car Care for the Clueless* specifically for older vehicle owners.)

Oakes was also recognized by AskPatty.com, a Web site that provides automotive advice for women. Pam's Motor City is designated a "Certified Female Friendly" service center.

Oakes' successful business has a staff that has been with the company for a long time. "There are techs who have been with my for 14, 12, 11 and 8 years," said Oakes Despite the rough economy, business is still fairly steady. "We remain very busy," she added.

Incident Management and the I-95 Corridor Coalition: An Interview with Capt. Tom Martin

I would like to just encourage you to get and stay involved. What you do is too important not to be recognized, but no one is going to do it for you. You are an industry of hard workers so work hard for you industry.

Remember, decisions about the future of private sector towing are being made every day and they will be made with or without you, so I encourage you get involved and get engaged.

— from Capt. Tom Martin's address to the TRAA Legislative and Leadership Conference, March 2011

Top-notch response time? An incident scene that is cleared quickly and efficiently? Smooth cooperation among first responders? These are key factors that are at the heart of traffic incident management — a topic that's an art as well as a science.

Tom Martin is well familiar with the intricacies of working an incident scene. A retired captain with the Virginia State Police, Martin works on traffic incident management and safety issues for the I-95 Corridor Coalition, an alliance of transportation agencies, toll authorities, and related organizations. Membership covers 16 states along the East Coast, from Maine to Florida — all of the states that are connected by Interstate 95.

Martin's popular address to the recent TRAA Legislative and Leadership Conference hit a lot of key points with regard to the towing industry's role in traffic incident management.

As key responders to incident scenes, towing and recovery personnel want — and need — to be viewed as equals among other experts tasked with clearing the roads.

"Over the years I've seen great improvement in how the towing and recovery industry is perceived," said Martin. "Many years ago law enforcement looked at towers as a necessarily evil. There wasn't much engagement except that the towers showed up at the scene and helped clear the accident."

Fortunately, added Martin, the relationship between law enforcement and towing took great strides as towers were asked to participate in training and other programs that helped improve incident management procedures.

The Coalition offers workshops dealing with subjects such as quick clearance. "Everyone's invited," said Martin. "We just had one of these workshops in Portland, Maine, and one in Connecticut." Of the 60 attendees, continued Martin, at least 10 people from 7 different towing companies were in the audience.

"It's so good when we have the towers there," said Martin, "because they can address their problems. Having them there to discuss their issues goes a long way in helping the other responders understand what's going on."

Pros on the road

Martin noted that the towing community's professionalism has blossomed over the past several decades. "It started with the Towing and Recovery Association of America," he explained. "They developed the Traffic Incident Management Handbook." That guide, said Martin, ensured that towers had information about incident management — and that they knew how to respond to various incidents on the road.

"As [towers] started to engage that concept, in most locations I've found that they're now an equal partner in traffic incident management, scene clearance and unified command," said Martin.

Despite this progress, Martin acknowledged that the attitude is not all pervasive and there's still progress to be made. "There are pockets of resistance everywhere," said Martin, "and problems with law enforcement too. But those problems are smaller than they used to be."

What is Martin's advice for towers who respond to incident scenes? "On a broad scale the greatest thing that towers can do is to work on the perception of professionalism," said Martin. Law enforcement agencies, he explained, consider themselves professional organizations. Most of them wear uniforms, for example, and their vehicles are well identified. The same goes for the fire department and personnel from the department of transportation.

Like those organizations, said Martin, the towing and recovery industry is group of professionals and should present itself that way: "It's important to be image-conscious. When they show up on scene, they should have some semblance of a uniform. It could be just a company t-shirt and nice slacks."

In addition, said Martin, tow vehicles should display a professional image, including a sharp paint job. "We see a lot where it's not that way," explained Martin.

Interpersonal communication is another key part of maintaining a professional image. "It's important that towers are engaging other responders — not only at scene but also prior to getting there."

27

A group effort

The I-95 Corridor Coalition has three staff positions: an operations program coordinator; a travel information service coordinator who archives traffic data; and the intermodal coordinator, who deals with truck parking and marine highways. "We tie all modes of transportation together," explained Martin, "whether it's rail, water, or ground."

The Coalition is funded by the Federal Highway Administration through its annual transportation authorization bill. "We don't buy anything. We don't sell anything. We don't tell anybody what to do or how to do it," said Martin. "We build consensus." Martin's role as the operations program coordinator is to supervise the organization's efforts with regard to incident management and safety.

For example: One topic that always pops up at the Coalition's workshops is the situation with local rotation lists. "You'll talk to agencies that have rotation lists, and they'll say the lists are fair," noted Martin. Sometimes, however, towers don't feel that way. Martin added that the Coalition tries to help agencies maintain balance out their rotation lists. "We meet with everyone and try to make sure it's a level playing field."

Joining the coalition

Martin's career with the Virginia State Police spanned an impressive 34 years. He began working with the I-95 Corridor Coalition in 1990, when the organization was formed. The Coalition staff is comprised of volunteers — many of whom are from law enforcement agencies.

As a state trooper, Martin attended the Coalition's meetings and events. He eventually segued into a leadership role, handling some of the organization's efforts in traffic incident management.

Martin's predecessor in the operations position was Henry deVries, a captain with the New York State Police, which loaned deVries to the Coalition full-time — a unique move during a time when the Coalition had only part-time volunteers. "Then the budget tightened up. NYSP called Henry back and the position was open," said Martin.

"Now the staff positions are funded," continued Martin, who eventually filled the vacated slot on the Coalition's staff. "It's an opportunity to do something different, and it keeps me engaged with the same people I dealt with when I was in law enforcement."

Martin has been in the position for more than two years. "I really enjoy it," he said. "It gives me a good opportunity to look at incident management and safety in this corridor." Prior to coming on staff at the Coalition, Martin said he primarily dealt with issues within the state of Virginia. "Now I can look at things from Maine to Florida and pick out best practices to make things better and safer."

"I never leave a conversation with anybody where we don't stress safety," said Martin, "safety for all responders — and that includes the towers. The clearance they provide, the equipment they bring, the lighting they bring — I think that towers bring a lot to the table when it comes to making the scene safer."

Photographing the World's Greatest Tow Trucks: The Life Journey of Earl Johnson

If you've read one of the eight volumes in the book series *The World's Greatest Tow Trucks*, you know that photographer Earl Johnson is an expert at turning tow trucks into stars. Johnson has spent three decades taking gorgeous photos of trucks of all types, including tow trucks. He compiles these photographs into books — so far, seven books about trucks, and eight about tow trucks. A new book is published every two or three years.

Before he became a photographer in the late 1970s, "I had a lot of different jobs," said Johnson. After he was discharged from the U.S. Army, Earl joined his father in selling wood-mounted, laminated photos of trucks.

Sometime after that, Johnson took a job as a truck driver. Things went fine until he had an accident, and decided that he "wasn't going to go back to driving."

Serendipity

At the time Johnson was living in Liberty, Texas. "The oil fields were going really strong," recalled Johnson, who planned to take photographs of the rigs and then mount the pictures on clocks to sell.

Suddenly everything changed — the rigs went bust. "That was one of the first big busts," said Johnson. "I got out to west Texas and nobody was drilling."

In 1982, Houston, Texas, tower Don Walters paid Johnson to take photographs of the company's tow trucks. "Then he told me about two or three other towers around Houston who wanted photos taken too," said Johnson, "so I did those."

"I was driving a pickup, had long hair and no money," recalled Johnson. Someone told him about the annual Florida Tow Show that was about to take place in Orlando. Why not head down there to drum up some business?

That sounded like a good idea to Johnson, who jumped in his pickup and drove to Florida. "I had a hundred dollars in my pocket and my pickup with blankets in the back," he said. Johnson planned to sell his "truck clocks" to people attending the gathering.

Once he reached the tow show, Johnson needed to find a place to pitch his wares. He saw Joe and Carol Gibney's booth for the *STA Phantom Towing News*, walked up to them and asked if he could sell his products at their table.

At first Gibney was quite reluctant. "She wasn't happy about sharing her booth, but she saw how people liked my photos. And by the end of that show, she had invited me to come to other shows!"

From that day Johnson began traveling to tow shows across the nation, selling his clocks along with belt buckles and other items.

Toughing it out

Johnson based his fledgling photography company out of Virginia Beach, Va. "My sister did my bookkeeping, and she lived there," explained Johnson. "I was on the road most of the time. I'd come home, kiss my three nieces, and sleep on the couch. Then I'd go back on the road, pulling into places where I could see if I could make a sale."

Several years later Johnson met his future wife, Grace, who encouraged his interest in photography.

But it was a family tragedy that forever linked Johnson with the towing and recovery industry.

A number of years ago Grace's son Dylan accompanied Johnson to the Chicago tow show. Johnson asked Dylan's permission to marry Grace, and Dylan — just nine years old at the time — gave his consent.

On the drive back from the show, headed home to Orlando, Johnson and Dylan were involved in an accident. Dylan didn't survive.

The moment they heard about the accident, towers nationwide reached out to help. The outpouring of support overwhelmed Johnson and Grace. "People in the towing industry came to our side like you would not believe," recalled Johnson. "That day, they became my family."

Standing his ground

During one of Johnson's road trips he met Ernie Vole, one of the legends of Chicago towing. "He was a tough character, and I still had my Texas accent," recalled Johnson. "People said, 'You're not going to be able to get anything from him. He hates vendors.'"

Johnson figured he had nothing to lose, so he visited Vole's office. "I still had a lot of red in my neck in those days," chuckled Johnson.

The word on Vole was dead-on accurate: Vole wasn't interested in buying photographs, he wasn't interested in hearing Johnson's sales pitch — and he made all of that very, very clear.

"He gave me a lot of s---," said Johnson. "So I said, 'F--- you, you S.O.B.!' and I left."

Then, to Johnson's amazement, "Ernie grabbed me by the collar and said, 'Come back in here and have a drink!'"

Johnson had passed the test. Vole liked to deal with people who could hold their own, especially when facing a challenge.

The two men shared a drink. Then Vole turned to Johnson. "What do you have to sell me?" Vole said.

"From that day on we were good friends," said Johnson.

The secret of photographing tow trucks

What makes Johnson's photographs stand out? And how does a photographer make a tow truck look good on camera?

"I don't keep secrets," said Johnson, who was happy to share the formula of taking great photos of tow trucks: "There really is no secret!"

The advent of digital photography has spoiled some photographers by making the process easier, said Johnson. While he's upgraded his equipment to the current digital standard, he still takes photographs the same way he always has: by trusting his eye and his intuition. "I like my shots to look simple — but it takes a lot of work to make it look that way," he explained.

Johnson's favorite type of shot is a "simple background," he said, "so that the truck is the main thing." He notes that if a photographer doesn't like trucks as stand-alone subjects, this will show in the photos that he or she takes because "they'll try to do fancy stuff or add things digitally" to enhance what they feel is an unexciting photograph.

Tiny features in a shot can make all the difference. Johnson recalled a recent photo shoot where, after Johnson had set up his camera on a tripod, the client looked through the viewfinder and then shifted the camera — just a little bit.

But in moving the camera setup, the client lost part of the shot that Johnson wanted to get. When Johnson checked the viewfinder again, he realized what had happened. He called the client over.

"That's not my shot," Johnson explained to the client. "You see that little glint on the chrome over there? If you move the camera, say, two inches, you lose that."

Some things are simple but not obvious, said Johnson. However, an experienced photographer has an innate "feel" for how to set up a great photograph. "Nowadays I usually do it without thinking about it," he explained.

Framing the shot is critical, Johnson continued. Some photographers don't plan their shot by focusing squarely on the subject — the truck itself. Instead, they make the mistake of looking at everything in the background of the truck, thinking that "everything has to be beautiful everywhere." That's not necessary, said Johnson, who encouraged photographers that "as soon as you put up the camera and look through the frame, nothing else exists."

No two photographers will take the same type of photo of the same tow truck, said Johnson. "The difference between the photos is the photographer's vision. People like what you do because of the way you present it."

Doing business

But the business isn't just about the technical side of things, said Johnson. "It's also about the relationships you build. You're not just selling books, or just photographs. You have to develop relationships with clients. I've spent 30 years doing that." This is especially important in a niche type of business such as taking photographs of tow trucks. There are only so many potential customers, so getting them — and keeping them — is critical.

In addition, clients must be willing to pay fair rates for good work, said Johnson. The first time Johnson negotiated his rate for a photography assignment, he was smart enough to establish a fair rate commensurate with his standards of quality.

"But the guy down the street charges less!" complained the client.

"Well," answered Johnson, "maybe you'd better use that guy, then."

"But I like yours better!" stammered the client.

Johnson held his ground — and got the gig.

New ideas

Johnson is always looking for ways to expand his product line. He recently offered collector's sets of newly printed hardcover editions of his books. "The collector's set was introduced at the Florida Show and offered in advance of publication to companies who have participated in the books over the years," said Johnson. "When the last set is sold there will be no more printed."

To spread the word about what he does, Johnson plans to design a new brochure that spotlights his photography business and his lineup of books.

Speaking of those books, Johnson is thinking about launching a new series where he would visit towing companies across the country and compile photographs of their tow trucks into individual volumes.

For that project Johnson may offer a special incentive: "If a towing company buys 100 of the books, they get their picture on the cover," he explained. "Then they can give that book out to local libraries, police departments, and schools. That way the book can be used as a public relations tool."

Back on the road

After three decades as a photographer, Johnson maintains a heavy travel schedule. He completed a new book of photos, *The World's Greatest Tow Trucks: Volume 8*. And he's started working on his next publication. When he's on the road, Johnson posts entries on his Web site to keep clients and fans up to date.

While Johnson loves what he does, he knows that — true to the old adage — most of his success is the result of perseverance and a lot of hard work. "Everybody thinks I have the best job in the world," said Johnson. "They don't know how hard it really is!"

'Tis the Season for Towers: Gift-Giving for the Holidays

The holidays are a time to celebrate, reflect, cherish — and, for many towers, a time to give and receive gifts. Whether they're giving gift certificates, food baskets, participating in "Secret Santa" gift exchanges, or participating in special activities in the community, employers and employees across the nation have both traditional and not-so-traditional methods of celebrating the season.

Gifts from boss to employee

Like many towing company owners, Earl Mumma, president of Highspire Auto & Truck Repair Corporation in Steelton, Penn., hosts a Christmas party for his employees. The company also gives out "bonuses for all amounts, depending on work performance throughout the year," said Mumma.

Some companies play Santa during the holidays, creating a "wish list" of the gifts that employees hope to receive. At Tony's Wrecker Service, Inc., in Louisville, Ky., owner Nick Schade takes a direct approach: "I tend to ask the employees what would they like Santa to bring them," he said. Schade's employees typically ask for tools, rain gear, flashlights, additional LEDs for their trucks — and that's just for starters.

Wish lists can vary depending on the employee and what vehicle he or she drives, said Schade. "I have been known to allow them to go on the tool truck and pick something within a price range," he added, "or get them a gift card for the tool truck."

Gift certificates are another popular holiday gift item. At Five Seasons Auto Rebuilders in Cedar Rapids, Iowa, owner David Beer hosts a party and hands out gift certificates to the entire staff, "so they can take their spouse out for a real nice supper or something like that," said Beer.

Holiday meals

What would the holidays be without large amounts of delicious food? Santa Fe Towing Service, headquartered in Lenxa, Kan., came up with an interesting twist on the classic holiday food basket.

"Each year," said Carrie Kupchin, vice president of the company, "we give all employees baskets filled with Christmas day meals for them to share with their families." But this isn't a basket full of fruit or nuts or some combination thereof. These baskets contain complete holiday meals.

Hopefully you're not hungry as you're reading this article, because we thought you'd like to know what the Kupchins place in each gift basket. Here goes: turkey or ham, stuffing mix, a bag of potatoes, a can of corn, a can of green beans, dinner rolls, pumpkin pie, whipped cream, hot cocoa, a dozen eggs, bacon, butter, cinnamon rolls, a bag of apples, and a bag of oranges.

Now that's one holiday basket that has it all. And it's a gift that the company has been giving to its employees for nearly 50 years.

What to put under the tree

Maybe you're looking for towing-themed gifts that are a bit out of the ordinary. Not that there's anything wrong with traditional selections, but we thought we'd list a few interesting alternatives for your gift list:

If your gift recipient loves books and tow trucks, visit www. earljohnsontruckbooks.com and check out the eight-volume series *The World's Greatest Tow Trucks*. Photographer Earl Johnson has spent the better part of three decades documenting tow trucks with his camera. Johnson's full-color photographs are captivating, and his popular books continue flying off the shelves every time he publishes a new volume.

The online store at the International Towing Museum offers everything from clothing to books, calendars, caps, Lego kits and baby clothing. (Of course, if you're in Chattanooga, Tenn., make sure you drop by the museum in person to check out their gift shop in person.)

Among the museum store's products is the blue Survivor Fund wrist bracelet, which costs just $2. All revenue from the sale of the bracelets goes directly to the towing industry Survivor Fund, established by the museum "to help the families of the men and women that have made the ultimate sacrifice in the line of service." The museum plans to raise half a million dollars for the Survivor Fund, which gifts $1,000 to eligible families of towers who have died in the line of duty.

My wish list

What do towing company owners and their staffs hope to receive for the holidays? Sometimes the answer is simple — and functional. At Tony's Wrecker Service, "We like wall calendars and scratch pads," said Schade. "Wall calendars because you can write information on them for schedule, vacation, and the like. Scratch pads because I don't allow the employees to use our company-printed pads because those are to be handed out to customers."

Schade added that the office staff at his shop likes the big barrels of popcorn that are typically sent during the holiday season. Why? "Well, because it is good!" he chuckles.

On his "wish list" Beer has an interesting gift idea for towing companies that have contracts with motor clubs. "What if the motor clubs provided a bonus to the [towing company] employees?" he explained. Since the motor clubs encourage towing companies to "be the best, have the best ETAs [estimated times of arrival], and have the best employees," said Beer, why shouldn't the motor clubs thank high-performing towers with year-end bonuses of some type?

This type of appreciation for a job well done applies equally to the customers. Beer recalled a towing job that he completed on a recent Christmas Day. When a motor-club customer got stuck in the snow, "I got a call at 7 a.m.," said Beer. "The customer was in a little town out west of Cedar Rapids [Iowa], about 10 miles away. There are no services out there."

When he received the call, Beer and his family were about to head out to visit relatives for the holidays. "Our car was in the driveway, loaded with packages, and we're headed to grandma's house," said Beer.

Beer delayed his family trip, hopped in his truck, and drove to the stranded customer's location. The stranded driver needed a jump-start, which Beer completed quickly. But even on Christmas Day, this particular customer wasn't in the holiday mood. "They jumped in their car and headed out," recalled Beer, "without even a thank you."

So what's the lesson learned from this experience? It doesn't take much time or effort to show some appreciation to a tower for a job well done — especially when the tower sacrifices his or her family time so that others can enjoy theirs.

The gift of giving

Some towing companies also offer gifts to their communities. One west coast towing company offers a gift card of a different stripe. "What we do is promote the 'don›t drink and drive' theme here in downtown Los Angeles," said Andrés (Andy) Dueñas, owner of United Carrier, Inc., Towing Services.

Dueñas and his staff hand out small cards to bars and other local businesses to be passed out to tenants and clients. "Are you going to drink and drive today?" reads the card. "If you are stopped drunk, it can cost you up to $10,000!" The card offers a five-mile tow for $39.

"We are part of RADD," said Dueñas, referring to the non-profit international organization that advocates the use of designated drivers, seatbelts, and safe driving. The Los Angeles-based division of the program launched several years ago and empowers celebrities, media partners, businesses and supporters to create positive attitudes about road safety.

United Carrier tows with clients such as the Automobile Club of Southern California, local auto dealerships and rental car agencies. During the holidays Dueñas and his staff usually pass out pastries to their vendors. The baked goods come from Portos Bakery & Cafe, a family-owned Los Angeles landmark founded in 1960.

Finally, sometimes a holiday gift isn't something you can hold in your hand, but something just as meaningful to your employees, customers, and their families and friends. When asked what he'd like to receive for the holidays, Earl Mumma made a simple wish: "Peace on Earth and good health for all."

Tornado Watch:
Towers Engage in Disaster Relief Efforts

From time to time, after a natural disaster has struck a community, towers from various companies band together to put the pieces back together. And that's when the phrase "towing and recovery" takes on a whole new meaning.

On May 22, 2011, a tornado struck the community of Joplin, Mo., and leveled the town. Towers responded immediately, in many different ways.

JOHN KUPCHIN AND SANTA FE TOW SERVICE: DEALING WITH THE AFTERMATH

Jon and Carrie Kupchin's company, Santa Fe Tow Service, is headquartered in Lenexa, Kan. The company has offices in Lenexa, Kan. (near Kansas City); Joplin, Mo., and Cedar Hill, Texas (a suburb of Dallas).

Jon Kupchin said that his crew is always ready to swing into action whenever local communities need towing and recovery services — especially after a natural disaster that leaves devastation and tragedy in its wake. "We've dealt with tornadoes in the past," said Kupchin. "One came through Kansas City. We moved maybe 200, 300 cars at that time. We've had floods where we've moved 800 to 1,000 cars."

A tornado that pounded Greensburg, Kan., in May 2007 crushed the city and killed 11 residents. "We were called upon by some insurance companies to go down and move equipment and stuff like that," recalled Kupchin. "So as far as moving volume, it's nothing that we can't handle."

On Sunday, May 22, 2011, one of the deadliest tornadoes in American history dropped onto the city of Joplin, Missouri — and wiped everything out.

A house divided

That afternoon the phone rang at the Kupchin home in Lenexa. Jon Kupchin had been spending a relaxing day watching television. He picked up the receiver. On the other end of the line was Rob Lane, the company's terminal manager in Joplin, Mo., a community of 50,000 people just 150 miles due south of Lenexa. Lane was getting ready to transfer to Dallas, where he would open the company's new branch office. He had put his house on the market the previous week.

"Well," said Lane, "I don't have to worry about selling my house anymore."

"Why is that?" said Kupchin.

"Because I just got hit by a fricking tornado!"

Kupchin couldn't believe it. "You've got to be kidding me," he said.

Kupchin switched on The Weather Channel — and got his first glimpse of the devastation in Joplin. "I saw it and thought, 'Oh my God, the whole town is just devastated,'" recalled Kupchin.

On the other end of the line, Lane described what he saw from his house as the twister approached. "I looked out my window and all I saw was black," said Lane. "When they say it sounds like a freight train, that's a true statement!"

Lane grabbed his dogs and crawled into a closet in the center of the

44

house. When the tornado blew through, it tore the roof off the house and knocked down the bedroom walls. Afterward only half of the structure remained standing.

But the crisis wasn't over. "I think what was the most damaging thing in that city was that after the tornado, it rained for two days straight," said Kupchin. "So anything that was damaged or if the roof was gone, all of the rain poured in, soaked all of the insulation and sheetrock, and all of that fell into the houses."

Swinging into action

After telling Lane that he'd get back to him, Kupchin dialed his dispatch office. He wanted to know if his tow trucks were being summoned to Joplin to pull vehicles out of the debris.

"Has anybody called from Joplin?" he asked.

"No," answered the dispatchers.

However, it didn't take long for this to change. Within five minutes, "the phones just blew up" with multiple calls from Joplin. But Kupchin couldn't talk to any of his staff and crew in that city — the tornado had knocked down all of the cell towers.

Kupchin didn't want to sit and wait, so he quickly notified his key personnel in the Kansas City area. "Let's go," he told them. "We've gotta go." Kupchin packed his bag, ran out of his house, jumped in the truck and drove straight through to Joplin. He was on the road for several hours and saw lots of nasty weather as he roared down the highway toward his destination.

Cleaning up

Vehicle owners, trucking companies and other drivers began calling Kupchin and his staff for help. "MODOT [Missouri Department of Transportation] called my cell phone from a satellite phone because they had no other communications," said Kupchin.

"We know you have several trucks you have to upright," the MODOT representative told Kupchin. "But we've got to get the highway open." Interstate Highway 44, a major east-west route, was a mess. Kupchin moved his trucks and equipment there, "and we cleaned the highway and got it open."

As he and his crew worked on the side of the highway, caravans of ambulances passed by. "It was just unbelievable how many people came to move people who were at the hospital or trapped in debris," said Kupchin.

As the insurance companies activated their crisis action teams and began hunting for missing vehicles, Kupchin received more phone calls. "Usually they want you to move straight from the scene to their [vehicle] pool," explained Kupchin," but their pool was 75 miles away." On an average day the pool might hold five cars from the Joplin area. After the tornado, the number of vehicles on the lot would swell to over 2,000.

Six weeks in Joplin

Kupchin stayed in Joplin for a month and a half, coordinating recovery efforts with his crews. He was limited by the debris left in the tornado's wake. "I can't go in there and just pick up cars and take them straight out on a two-car [carrier], and I can't get transporters or four-car haulers into areas where the cars are," he recalled. He used whatever equipment would do the job. "We did it with our rotators and any wrecker we had." At the peak of the operation, Santa Fe Tow Service had 17 trucks on site.

"We were moving over 150 cars from the disaster area each day," said Kupchin. "Our multi-cars were delivering four loads a day, anywhere from seven to 10 cars per load. I had six of those multi-cars running, and 11 light-duty trucks bringing cars in."

One of the biggest challenges for the tow truck drivers was locating missing vehicles. "The assignments would have an address, but the vehicles — boats, trailers, vans, RVs, box trucks —were seldom there," said Kupchin. "Cars were wedged in trees, on top of houses, underneath houses, and sometimes blocks away. Depending on the location of the vehicle, our heavy-duty fleet would often assist the light-duty drivers recovering the vehicles from the debris."

Office manager Misty DeGonia played a huge role in the recovery efforts. She had grown up in Joplin and recruited local residents to act as guides, riding along with the tow truck drivers. This was especially helpful because the tornado had blown away street signs across the city. "Every time drivers came back to the office for their next assignment, Misty and her office staff made sure they stayed fed, hydrated, and motivated," said Kupchin.

Kupchin personally loaded the transporters at the staging area for rescued vehicles. "That's all I did, all day long, from six in the morning until dark," he recalled. "At one time we had over 275 cars in the yard, because the light-duty trucks were bringing them in faster than we could get them out."

During the six-week operation Kupchin and his crew slept in a makeshift camp and in their trucks — there were no motel rooms available.

Looking back

The spirit of cooperation among the various recovery workers greatly impressed Kupchin. "We worked around the debris trucks, and the debris trucks worked around us. We worked around the power company, and the power company worked around us."

At one point the power company needed to lay a replacement line, but a giant pile of obstacles blocked the workers from accomplishing the job. "There were 17 trailers upside down and on top of each other," said Kupchin. "We had to get those trailers out of the way. So everybody just knuckled down and got the job done."

Four months after the tornado screamed through the city of Joplin, Kupchin and his company were still recovering property in the area. "We're still moving cars — not as many, but the Army Corps of Engineers is still digging out cars that have no insurance." Those cars are placed in the street, where the local police department uses 10 towing companies on a rotating basis to hook up and take the vehicles away.

It was an incredible operation in the middle of a completely devastated area. Now, just as then, Kupchin and his crew are ready to help if a natural disaster sweeps through a nearby community. "There was plenty of work for everybody," said Kupchin. "There was more work than people could handle. But we all got through it together."

MIKE SCOTT AND THE MISSOURI TOW TRUCK ASSOCIATION: MOVING A WATER PARK

Mike Scott — owner of Scotty's Carriage Works, Inc., in Cameron, Mo., and a member of the Missouri Tow Truck Association (MTTA) — noticed that the city of Fort Scott, Kan., had placed two water slides up for sale online. Fort Scott was about to demolish and rebuild its public water park, and it was unloading its used equipment.

"The MTTA was looking to do something to help out the people in Joplin after the F5 tornado rolled through the town," explained Scott. "Because the park is located across the street from the hospital that was destroyed, all structures around the pool including the lifeguard stands and diving boards were also gone. Even the water was virtually sucked completely out of the pool!"

Scott thought that the water slides could prove useful in Joplin, where families rattled by the tornado deserved a gift that could be enjoyed by the community.

However, there were two catches: Fort Scott had already contracted with a company to demolish the pools that had the slides, so the slides would have to be removed within a one-week period after the summer season was over. In addition, the slides were still bolted in place and needed to be picked up and moved — and Fort Scott would not be responsible for the expense. "That's how the MTTA could help," said Scott.

To bring the water slides to Joplin, Scott needed to assemble a group of volunteers. He picked up the phone and called Tom Watson of Mel's Tow Service in Kansas City, Mo., to discuss the possibility of buying and moving the slides. After talking to the parks and recreation department in Joplin, Watson and Scott were told that Fort Scott wanted to donate the slides to Joplin. All that was needed was someone to disassemble and transport the equipment.

Room to move

On a bright September morning, 15 volunteers from nine different towing companies got together in Fort Scott.

Jon Kupchin, owner of Santa Fe Tow Service in Lenexa, Kan., was one of the volunteers, along with several of his staff members. "Mike Scott called me and asked if I'd be willing to donate trucks plus a rotator to move the water slides. My company has a presence in Joplin, and I'll do anything to donate to recovery efforts after what's happened in that city."

"I supplied a 75-ton rotator to move the water slide," continued Kupchin, "plus a dry van trailer to move it in so it wouldn't have to be strapped down."

Mike Scott brought his Bobcatloader. "That little thing has a teleboom that extends something like 17 feet outward," he said. "We also brought a flatbed and a trailer. I knew that the teleboom on the Bobcat could get into small areas, to maneuver and pick up things and hand them off to the rotator." After that the, rotator would swing around and hand off the items to the flatbed or trailer.

In addition to moving the water slides, the volunteers transported additional donated equipment such as diving boards, lifeguard stands, and pool pumps.

Organized this way, the operation went smoothly. "This way somebody was doing something all the time," explained Scott. "While several guys were unbolting and disassembling the next piece, other guys were disassembling the pumps. In the kiddie pool there were two slides that were red, like the slides you see at McDonald's. The guys disassembled those."

With all of the equipment loaded up, the volunteer crew drove the water slides to Joplin, where the parks and recreation department stored them in several holding facilities. That winter — when the parks weren't too busy — the parks department planned to sand down the fiberglass slides and have a local company refinish the surfaces with a fresh layer of gelcoat. Then, during the spring, the slides would be installed at pools in Joplin.

The project was another good example of towers making a difference in their communities, above and beyond their regular daily work. "We try to give back to the industry and we try to find good things to do in our communities," said Scott.

Getting the Dough to Keep the Shop Running: Finance in a Time of Distress

Since tow trucks are the heart and soul of this industry, the rocky national economy — which in 2007 plunged into a recession that ended in 2009, according to the National Bureau of Economic Research — took an axe to many towers' credit status and subsequently their ability to obtain financing for truck and equipment purchases. The situation was so dire that industry vendors were having difficulty selling tow vehicles and large pieces of equipment.

The nation's financial situation "has left many towers — and businesses in general — looking not as strong financially," said Vincent Diglio, chief financial officer of Channel Islands Leasing & Loan in Ojai, Calif. The company provides financing for commercial equipment and specializes in trucks and trailers.

With lenders keeping a tight hold on their purse strings, towers aren't getting the financing they need to keep their businesses rolling, and dealers are having trouble moving their inventories. "The economic downturn has dealt a fatal blow to many companies, while inflicting significant damage to others," noted Amanda Adolf, owner of Preferred Towing in Castaic, Calif. "The survivors are now looking at ways to boost their bottom lines to reach profitability goals."

Tight purse strings in a tough economy

After a credit-crazy period where— thanks to a housing boom driven by easy lending — it seemed like almost anyone could obtain financing, things have changed dramatically. "It is tough to find available capital in the current market," said Adolf. Many banks and financial institutions are now out of business and counting their losses from failed sub-prime endeavors, she added. "Banks and lenders that do have money to lend have severally tightened their credit requirements, leaving many business owners unable to qualify for traditional financing."

Jeffrey Godwin, vice president of FTI Groups, Inc., and towXchange, Inc., has kept careful watch over the financial market and its effect on the towing industry. Although things are rough right now, Godwin provides some hopeful advice. He points to three possible options available to towers: cash, leasing, and financing with their banks. "Strong relationships with banks are a great resource but may want to be saved for miscellaneous operating expenses," said Godwin. "If a company needs basic operating cash and they have already used their line of credit, it can put them in a tight spot."

Leasing is probably the best option in most cases, continued Godwin, because "it is set for an exact amount, for an exact amount of time, and provides stability in business operations."

Adolf, who founded her California towing business in 1998, agrees. "Equipment leases provide some of the most flexible commercial financing terms available today," she said. "While businesses struggle to avoid a fatal blow, equipment leasing may offer some relief."

Bolstering credit status

Diglio notes that financial firms understand the difficulties that towers are facing. "So we try to look past the financials of last year to what›s happening now," he said.Diglio points to two areas where towers can help make themselves appear stronger financially — and, ultimately, more creditworthy.

The first thing to do, according to Diglio, is to keep as much money in the company bank account as possible. Financial firms look at current bank statements when determining the creditworthiness of a client. "If we›re looking to see if a company has weathered the storm, we don't want to see that they just have $68 in their account," noted Diglio.

A second thing that financial firms scrutinize is a tower's credit card situation. "We look at the amount of money that is owed on credit cards," said Diglio. "In the finance world, anything about $20,000 is considered a red flag."

For example, if a towing company owner is carrying $50,000 on his or her credit cards, "we're going to be wondering how a tower can afford a new truck if he can't pay down his credit card debt," explained Diglio.

Godwin agrees. "First and foremost," he said, "understand your credit. A lot of customers don't stay on top of their credit enough to understand. A simple small collections account can really drive down the possibility of getting the best rates — and even getting financed," added Godwin.

Alternatives to leasing

For towers who don't want to lease, what else is there? "For towers who are credit-challenged, a loan or lease doesn't make a difference," said Diglio. "It'll be the structured terms that'll matter. For instance, how much money they are asked to put down." Diglio notes that most finance companies may prefer to use a lease contract with a customer who is credit-challenged. This arrangement provides more protection to the finance company, just in case the tower has difficulty paying the bills.

Although as a leasing and loan expert Diglio leaves picking a type of contract up to the tower's accountant, he does have some thoughts on the matter. "Ever since 2001 the IRS has allowed for bonus depreciation methods that may favor loans over true leases," said Diglio.Times certainly have changed. "Prior to 2001," explained Diglio, "90 percent of our business was in loans," he said. "But since then we've been writing 90 percent of our contracts as loans."

Resources for the greater good

If towers need advice or information about what to do, a number of good resources are easily available. Some of these resources can help towers get a loan — or just plan to apply for one in the future. "Reach out to associations and other organizations that you might be a part of," urges Godwin. "Fellow colleagues who have used specific services will have great advice."

Godwin also recommends that towers touch base with industry organizations like towPartners. Established in the late 1990s, towPartners was designed to bring better pricing and quality service benefits to towing and road service companies of all sizes and to those employed in the industry.

In addition, said Godwin, towPartners has linked up with Direct Capital, a financing company based in Portsmouth, N.H., to provide leasing solutions for towPartners members. Direct Capital, which has loaned over $1 billion during its 17-year history, provides financial products such as capital loans, equipment financing and merchant cash advances.

Even if you're afraid of being turned down, don't be afraid to talk directly to financial companies, says Diglio. "I would have to plug my company, Channel Islands Leasing & Loan," said Diglio, "and [encourage towers to] speak to one of our representatives."

However, if a client is "really credit challenged," said Diglio, "the government has incentivized the community banks ... to give loans by guaranteeing the loans up to 75 percent from funds allocated out of the bailout fund." Because of the federal backstop, Diglio explained, clients should expect community banks to be more aggressive in approving loans. However, people must remember that there is no mandate and the banks are free to make their own choices as to whether to give loans to customers.

A brighter future?

Despite the gloomy economy, the financial experts with whom we talked are hopeful as they look down the road. "My outlook for the future is good, but progress will occur at a slower pace," said Diglio. "There is no quick remedy to remove this country›s deficit, and there isn›t a quick fix for the construction industry which used to drive a good portion of the economy."

However, added Diglio, with foreclosure stocks dwindling over time, development and construction will come back slowly, just as the economy will. All of this activity will in turn trigger reductions in the federal deficit. And that's good for everyone.

So even in this financial climate — and perhaps lacking very strong credit — should a wary tower go after a loan for new trucks and equipment? By taking the advice of good money experts and watching your credit and bank account closely, you might just get that financing you need to add a new tow truck or equipment to your company.

Collections: Getting What's Owed

Unfortunately, there are times when vehicle owners are — for various reasons — uninterested in reclaiming their towed property from an impound lot and paying off the bill. To avoid having towed vehicles stacked like cordwood in the lot, it's helpful for lot owners to send unclaimed property to auction, where they can attempt to retrieve some of the money that's owed to their company.

At Retriever Towing in Portland, Ore., owner Gary Coe said that he's fortunate: "We have very few receivables that we have to chase." However, added Coe, "we actively pursue the collection of deficient balances on lien sale cars."

When a vehicle is sold at auction, and the proceeds do not cover theamount owed for towing, storage, lien fees, and cost of the sale, Coe and his staff take the next step: they turn over the balance owed to a collection company.

Sometimes revered and sometimes reviled, collection agencies have a

57

tough job: convince the vehicle owner to settle what's owed to the towing company.

While collection agencies prefer to operate quietly and without fanfare, given the nature of their work, several of these organizations graciously agreed to talk about their relationships with towing companies and vehicle owners — and what towers need to know before they engage a collection company.

Types of collections for towers

"We collect on the storage and towing fees for towing companies as reflected on the lien sale," said Jenee McCray, operational manager for AAA Credit Service Collection Agency in Anaheim, Calif.

Added Keith Baker, CEO of Lien Enforcement, Inc., based in San Jose, Calif., "These are the vehicles — commonly referred to as Private Property Impounds (PPI) — which are typically towed at either law enforcement's request or by a third party such as an apartment complex manager."

While most of the collection agencies' business comes from towing companies submitting their lien-sold vehicles for collections, the collectors can chase other towing bills as well. At Credit Bureau Associates in Fairfield, Calif., President Kathy Parsons noted that her company also collects from companies "that owe [the towing company] money who may have had a contract with them to do multiple tows and don't pay the tow company invoice."

Lien Enforcement, Inc., "also helps towing companies with other types of debt that are less common," said Baker. These debts include charge-backs from credit cards, bad checks, personal loans to employees, roadside services that go unpaid, and "any other type of debt that the towing business may incur."

Retrieving money owed

Before considering whether to transfer an outstanding account to a collection agency, towing company owners should work the problem as much as possible.

Coe offered some tips to his fellow towing company owners: First, review accounts receivable every month or more often. "Make phone calls or assign a staff person to make phone calls to any account out over 45 days," explained Coe. Also make sure that the customer has a copy of the invoice, since "I don't have the invoice" is a common excuse.

Then, continued Coe, "Ask them specifically when you might expect payment. You may even ask if you can stop by to pick up the check. When they claim that 'the check is in the mail,' make a note to call back if, after some time, the check appears to be '*lost* in the mail' instead."

Baker offers several options that towing companies can use: send the delinquent vehicle owner an amnesty letter to settle the account before collections, send a balance due letter after the lien has expired, and negotiate settlements or offer a settlement.

Also, said Baker, "be sure the staff is trained to engage the consumer in the collection efforts by phone or at the counter, so the entire tow company is involved in recovering as much as possible before collection."

"We expect towing companies to do their diligence by making sure they notify the registered owner of their car being towed," said McCray. "Also, we expect them to make sure they have the correct registered owner." (However, added McCray, her company does not expect towers to send the collection agency any notifications other than the Notice of Lien Sale.)

Handing the ball to a collections agency

Collection agencies have a variety of tools at their disposal when attempting to get customers to settle their bills. Parsons and her staff of 36 employees receives "daily reports if the consumer moves, shops for new credit, buys a home, etc.," said Parsons. "Our skip tracing staff looks for social security numbers on each account and verifies spelling of names so we know we are looking for the correct person."

For towing company owners, having gathered as much information as possible about the vehicle and its owner is a huge timesaver when the account is transferred to a collection agency. According to Parsons, "The collection agency can help the tow company better if they have this information up front because of disputes and requests for verification of the debt by the consumer that the collection agency must by law respond to. Also, if legal action is started the agency already has the paperwork."

According to McCray, the collections agency needs the registered owner's information, the date the car was towed and sold, how much the car was sold for at lien sale (or how much they got for it being junked), and the type of car.

Towers can take a look inside the vehicle to gather documentation about its owner. "It's amazing what a quick check of the driver compartments and glove box could garner," said Dennis Wencel, author of *The Black Book of Towing*. "Pay stubs, registration statements and other personal documents will help your agency make contact with the responsible party. It always amazed me what type of information people will carelessly leave in their now-abandoned vehicle."

Also, said Baker, "If a consumer picks up personal items from the stored vehicle, have them sign over the car and negotiate on the balance due. At the same time have the consumer complete a personal property recovery form." This form should include room for a work number, home phone, cell phone, job and company for which the customer works, and current address. If the customer fails to pay the towing company, this information will be useful when engaging a collections agency.

Success rates

On average, the agencies we talked to estimated the success rate for collections at anywhere between 1 and 10 percent, depending on the particulars of a specific account.

Parsons noted that this percentage is lower than the average of any other industry and depends on the assets of the consumer and the demographics involved. Collection agencies can report the account for seven years to the national credit reporting databases and, if necessary, sue the delinquent customer for payment. However, added Parsons, "collection agencies cannot pull a credit report on the consumer unless they have a money judgment, so [they] must use other skip tracing tools to locate assets such as home ownership and employment data."

A tough economy and the fickleness of human beings also affect the success rate of collection companies. For example, people who no longer own their vehicle are obviously less inclined to pay for a car that they no longer drive. "In my experience," noted McCray, "most people do not want to pay the fees until it is placed on their credit, affecting their ability to get a loan, buy a house/car, et cetera."

"You will typically get many more unpaid accounts when the economy is down," said Wencel, "and conversely you will see payments of these accounts increase as people are attempting to dig themselves out of a financial hole as the economy improves."

It may take time and effort to collect, but that effort can be worth the trouble. "While [collections agencies] actually only get a small percentage of those they chase," said Retriever Towing's Gary Coe, "it does bring in $500 to $10,000 per month that we would otherwise not receive."

According to Parsons, "Tow companies that recover the most money are willing to settle to get the account collected and will tell their agency what their comfort zone is on settling accounts."

Also, said Parsons, the tow company that maintains good recordkeeping usually sees a higher recovery "since the account is on the credit report for seven years and we never know when a new phone number or address or job is found."

Choosing a collections agency

So if you've been unable to get a vehicle owner to pay an outstanding bill, how can you choose a reputable collections agency to help you with the problem?

According to Parsons, tow companies should always use an agency that reports to all the national credit bureaus and is willing to pay for access to skip tracing databases. "Also," said Parsons, "they should ask for a status report on their accounts and communicate with their collection agency for optimum results."

"As with all legal matters, said Wencel, "be sure you consult your attorney and review and comply with your state's laws to understand what is allowable under the collections process. For example, Illinois limits the quantity of storage days you can submit into collections to thirty."

A good collections agency should be polite, persistent, and willing to work with the delinquent client to settle the debt fairly. "Towing companies should know that we specialize in the industry and are very experienced in collecting towing fees from their former clients," said McCray.

"We are always open to working with the tow companies," said Parsons. "The economy the last few years has not been great, as we all know, but if the tow company is working with a ethical and strong collection agency they will see results."

Getting the information ready

Keith Baker, CEO of Lien Enforcement, Inc., offers a checklist of what towers should do when they run into a collection problem:

1. First and foremost, the vehicle owner must be notified that the vehicle was impounded. Each state has its own laws that define the process of proper notification.

2. Unclaimed vehicles that have cleared the lien sale process must be disposed of, either by sale at auction to the general public or to the junkyard prior to being submitted for collections. The money received from the sale of the vehicle (if any) needs to be applied to the remaining balance due. The deficient amount remaining can then be submitted for collections.

3. Gather as much information about the customer as possible. When customers come into towing companies to pick up their personal property from the vehicle, this is a clear sign that the person is not returning for their vehicle. It is the best opportunity for towing company owners to gather information such as a copy of the driver's license, phone numbers, date of birth, social security number, and correct mailing address. Most of this information can be obtained by simply handing the customer a "Property Release Form" which could include this information as questions on it.

4. Each state has rules and regulations about what can be requested from the registered owner when they come in for personal property, as well as what cannot be requested. Any information that the towing company owners request should first be reviewed by an attorney or the city contractor they work for.

Ultimately, the more information that towing company owner

gathers about the customer, the greater their chances of collecting the account themselves — as well as assisting their collection agency with recovering the debt.

Quick tips on collecting

According to Kathy Parsons, president of Credit Bureau Associates in Fairfield, Calif., "Tow companies should provide their collection agency a copy of the lien packet which includes the pending lien sale, DMV printout and certification of mailing, along with a copy of the invoice showing credit for sale of car or vehicle."

— Know when to chase and when to let it go. Gary Coe of Retriever Towing in Portland, Ore., pointed to a certain motor club that sometimes shorts payment of invoices — and sometimes ignores those invoices completely. Would it be worth a tower's time and trouble to go after the money owed? In Coe's case, the answer is no. "We would be wasting our time to turn those over to a collector," said Coe.

— Whenever there's some quiet time in your office, it's an opportunity to make some calls to vehicle owners who owe you money. "The collections process can initially be a bit confusing," said Dennis Wencel, author of *The Black Book of Towing*. "But once you've automated the process, it becomes quite easy and serves as great filler work for office staff and dispatcher downtime."

Processing Credit Cards for Your Towing Business

Cash, check or credit? These days credit cards are ubiquitous, and processing them is convenient for the customer as well as the towing company — as long as the system is set up correctly.

If you're just beginning to accept credit cards, you'll need to choose *how* to process transactions: By swiper in the shop? By hand held processing device? Or maybe your drivers can use their smart phones while they're on the road?

The last option — using smart phones to process credit card sales — is the latest technology on the market. "We have seen a growing popularity with towing companies using smart phones to accept and process credit cards in real time securely," said Ken Lewis, supervisor at Paymentmax Merchant Services, one of the many companies that process credit card transactions for towing companies.

Whether you're just beginning to offer credit card processing or have been at it for a long time, it pays to take a closer look at practical ways to make sure you're getting the most bang for your buck.

Setting it up

First and foremost, do your homework when hunting for a credit card processing service. "I like to keep it simple!" said Amanda Adolf, owner of Preferred Towing in Castaic, Calif. Having your bank process your credit cards is convenient, noted Adolf, but convenience can come at a price. "There are literally hundreds of credit card processing companies; shop the market! I received quotes from third-party processors, and then returned to my bank to see if they could match the rate, or lose a customer. Needless to say, my bank was willing to match the rates."

"For the best transaction rates and fees," said Michelle Jones of Simple Merchant Services, "the motto is, 'Shop often and avoid long contracts.'"

While you're shopping around, see if you can find discounts, said Susan Totman of Totman Enterprises, Inc., in Belmont, Maine. If you tow for auto clubs such as AAA, explained Totman, ask them if they have any programs that offer discounts with merchant services, which can make a big difference at the end of the month.

Although many online vendors are interested in doing business with towers, Nick Schade of Tony's Wrecker Service in Louisville, Ky., likes to stay local for his credit card processing. "I would say go to your bank and set it up with the local branch," said Schade. "Deal with a well known local bank. They tend to give better rates because they have a lot more clients in the merchant services area already."

Schade feels that staying local gives your hometown bank more "hometown business." By working with your local bank on credit cards, you may find yourself with stronger "buying power" during those times when you need to apply for a bank loan.

Keeping costs down

If you don't already accept credit cards, should you start? The towing company owners we queried had a common answer: "Do it," said Totman. "The ability to accept credit cards gives you access to many, many more customers than you can begin to realize."

Totman added that many towing companies are wary of transaction fees and therefore still don't accept credit cards from their customers. But "paper checks are on the way out and there are a great many people nowadays who carry limited or no cash at all," explained Totman. "They [use] cards for almost every expense, large or small."

"With all the demands of running a business," said Adolf, "shopping for competitive rates and understanding processing fees might seem trivial; however, a healthy dose of due diligence can go a long way."

According to Adolf, understanding processing fees can save or cost hundreds or even thousands of dollars. "For example," said Adolf, "with most processors, actually swiping the card (rather than punching in the number) results in a lower processing fee." Talk to your processor, added Adolf, and make sure you fully understand the fees and process.

What about towing company owners who aren't happy about paying fees? Factor those fees into the towing chargesas appropriate to cover your administrative expenses, said Totman.

As a tower, Bill Johnson — owner of Hampshire Towing in Granby, Mass. — appreciates the protection that credit cards provide. "The bottom line with credit cards is a swiped transaction with a signature is almost impossible for customer to dispute and win. I have five mobile credit machines and charge a two-dollar airtime fee per transaction to offset the monthly charge."

Choosing a merchant provider

For towing company owners who haven't begun to offer credit card processing, Susan Totman recommends that they look at things from the customers' point of view. "Do not penalize customers because they are using a credit card," offered Totman. "Many companies add a percentage if customers pay via credit card. This is not only inappropriate and anti-productive in our opinion, but is generally against your agreement with your credit card processing company/bank, and you could face penalties or suspension/cancellation of your account."

When considering a processor, said Adolf, service and speed are important items to consider. "Most times, terms are also negotiable," explained Adolf, "so knowledge is your best weapon." Finally, she said, be cautious when committing to an agreement. Commonly, agreements run at least three years and carry hefty termination fees.

To keep a good relationship with your credit card processor, keep your financial data up to date, said Mike Patellis, owner of Alpha Towing in Marietta, Ga. "This will almost always prevent questions from the credit company about an unusually high or rarely-charged amount when a high charge is processed," said Patellis. The credit card processor, he added, likes to know that the towing company can cover a chargeback if it happens.

Volume, types of transactions, and types of credit cards all dictate your costs, said Schade. "Certain types of credit cards charge an additional service fee to the merchant to take their cards," Schade added. "We do not accept these types of cards for that reason."

At Alpha Towing, Patellis charges an extra $6 to the customer to process any card under $100, and charges an extra $12 for transactions over $100. Patellis reminds everyone that American Express charges a transaction fee of 3 percent, which can add quite a lot on top of an expensive towing invoice.

Schade's towing company, Tony's Wrecker Service, makes it a point to contact its merchant services provider each year to ensure that Tony's continues to receive the best rate possible. Although Tony's talks to other providers, the company has stayed loyal to its credit card provide for 12 years and counting.

Patellis agrees: "Stay with your credit card company," he said. "Don›t switch often for the better rate. Your credit card company will give you loyalty discounts over time."

"Merchant services is just like the towing business," explained Schade. "Someone will always do it cheaper, but remember: you get what you pay for."

Technology good and bad

Here's a unique situation: Johnson, a towing company owner, also owns a credit card processing company, Simple Merchant Services. Michelle Jones provided some behind-the-scenes information about the use of personal cell phones to process credit cards while on the road.

Although it's an enticing proposition, the appeal of the "most current technology" can be a trap, said Jones. That "current technology" — using smartphones such as the iPhone and Android to process credit card transactions — "is fast, convenient, mobile, and secure at the gateway. For drivers and owners this option at first glance looks like a win/win situation. Their drivers are mobile and so too are their processing needs."

But for some companies, added Jones, cell phone processing can be a potential hassle and a security risk. The weakness in the system, she said, is that any driver can upload the application into his or her cell phone and have direct access to the account simply by entering the pass code provided by the owner.

Jones cautions that while mobile processing seems great at the outset — lower terminal costs for the towing company owner, and the ability for drivers to process credit cards on the go — a number of possible security holes exist.

"The driver takes the application wherever he or she goes," explained Jones. "Even home, where credit card information can be easily stolen. The owner may have trust in the driver at the job, but does he/she know his/her whole family?"

Another important consideration is the cost involved. While it may be great that tow truck drivers can use cell phones to process credit cards, the bill for cell phone service will increase. Are tow company owners willing to take on the added expense of providing cell phones to all of their drivers? Moreover, when a driver quits or is terminated, the company needs to change all of the pass codes. This can eat up a lot of time, said Jones.

So what other options exist? Jones recommends the wireless terminal. "There is the cost of the terminal and air time," she says. But on the other hand, the terminal stays within the company's oversight, drivers can come and go without needing to change pass codes, and overall security increases.

"And," said Jones, "the airtime fee can be charged to the client, allowing the owner to recoup the fee and cost of the terminal."

Here to stay

The biggest goal of the credit card industry, said Jones, is lowering risk. "A majority of the increased costs in the industry are risk related," she explained. If the towing company owner takes consistent steps to lower the risk of theft and chargeback, he or she will see cost savings on the company's credit card statements.

Credit cards are here to stay, said Schade. "Cash is out there but not as widely used as before. I believe that a towing service that doesn't accept credit cards is passing up the opportunity for expanded business. More and more commercial accounts are paying with credit cards, which boosts volume and gives you a better rate."

"The bottom line," said Adolf, "is that yes, accepting credit cards costs a little bit, but the rewards in the increased sales volume are well worth the trouble and expense."

Four steps to credit card success

Susan Totman of Totman Enterprises in Belmont, Maine, offers the following tips for ensuring that your credit card transactions are smooth and convenient:

1. *Always* get a signature on both a road service receipt showing specific service provided *and* a signature on the slip from the credit card processing machine. We have had several occasions when a customer tried to charge back the towing fees. We had to provide proof that not only did the customer sign the charge slip, but that he or she also signed something authorizing the service. Each time we won because we had both signatures and had clearly identified the services provided. Compare signatures on the back of the card. If it's not signed, check their driver's license to ensure it's the customer's card.

2. Definitely get either a handheld terminal or credit card sliders for your cell phone (Android, iPhone, etc.) if your merchant has the service available. We prefer the handheld devices as they connect via satellite and don't necessarily depend on whether or not we have a cell phone signal. By contrast, the sliders connected to the cell require that you have a cell

phone signal to process. We can process payments almost anywhere with our handhelds.

3. Periodically ask for a rate comparison from competitive merchants, then go back to your credit card company with those quotes — they will generally be lower than your current rates. Your credit card company will almost always match the new lower rates offered by the other companies.

4. If for some reason you take a credit card transaction over the phone instead of sliding the card in the machine, make sure you get all of the customer's information, including name, address and telephone associated with the card, expiration, CSV [number] on the back of the card, and zip code. Try to get a signed credit card authorization — e-mail or fax it to the customer, and have him or her send it back. This can be challenging if you're on the road, but it can be very important because cards taken over the phone are risky. We are careful with whom we allow to do that. If we have concerns we get cash or check.

Credit card tips

A grab bag of quick tips from Mike Patellis, owner of Alpha Towing, Inc., in Marietta, Ga.:

The more info you gather for the credit card company — everything on the card, Zip code, street, etc. — the better the card rate you'll be charged.

The less info you gather from the customer, the higher the rate. Failure to get a billing address or exact name on card (including middle initial) results in a higher rate.

Keep your software up to date. We run everything on one PC — very safe, very secure.

We run everything as it comes in — no delay or waiting until end of day. Do it now.

Nothing is ever printed with a credit card number on it.

Be sure you are in compliance with Federal credit card processing rules, including privacy act restrictions.

Only allow a very few people to operate your credit card processing software.

Always be honest with the customer about what is going on the card, even if it's a $6 or a $25 admin fee. If you tell the customer, everyone is happy. If you don't the customer may dispute the charge — even if it's just $6!

If you must refund a customer, write a check. Don›t charge back or reverse the sale. This affects your rates and credit rating with the credit card company.

We video the operator of the computer that runs the credit card software in our shop.

If you don't take credit cards, you're losing a ton of business — if you're still *in* business!

I'd rather take a credit card over a check any day.

What To Do with a Worn-Out Card

Like many towers, Amanda Adolf, owner of Preferred Towing in Castaic, Calif., has had those days when a customer hands her a beat-up credit card whose magnetic strip has seen better days. What can you do? Let's see what Adolf says:

Most processors prefer for the business to actually swipe the card and can even charge less for doing so. At times, the strip on the back of the credit card may become unreadable and make it difficult to swipe. Here are a few tricks I picked up over the years to ensure that the credit card will swipe and I save the most in processing fees:

1. The Plastic Bag: Wrap the card in a thin, clear plastic bag and swipe it again. Using a plastic bag stretched over the strip helps to create more distance between the card and the machine's canal, and helps the machine to scan the card quickly and blur the damaged parts into the original reading.

2. Scotch Tape: Much the same as above, except use Scotch tape in place of a plastic bag. Apply a strip of Scotch tape over the magnetic strip of the back of the card, then swipe.

3. Give it a Licking: Probably the nastiest thing I have ever seen, but it does work. No, I do not know from experience — I would rather pay the higher rate than lick someone's credit card! But I have seen it done, and it does work.

72

Equipment Improvements for Better Towing

Over the last century — since that important day in 1916 when Ernest Holmes, Sr., rigged up his first makeshift tow truck — continuous innovations in technology have spurred critical changes in the towing and recovery industry. "Since I started in the industry we've gone from regular, mechanical Holmes winch trucks to big hydraulic 75-ton rotator trucks," noted Todd Suhr, parts manager at Zip's Truck in New Hampton, Iowa. "And now we also have those big side-pullers you can install on your truck, so towers don't take up to or three lanes of traffic while they're recovering a vehicle."

But it's not just technology that's altering the way towers approach their work — there's also a change in mindset. The majority of towers we talked to mentioned new safety procedures and equipment as two of the most important "innovations" in recent years. But it's not just about reflective clothing and a renewed sense of caution — it's also about new gear that helps *create* a safer on-the-job environment.

While the "old school" ways of towing are still very much alive, advancements in equipment design have revolutionized the industry in recent years. The local tow operator might still pull up in an old truck, wrap chains around the wheels, and accept only cash payments. But these days, you're more likely to see a bright LED-lit wrecker sporting a fifth wheel underlift, with a driver working with a wireless credit card processing device, updated straps and alloy snatch blocks, among other items.

Wheels up

At Totman Enterprises in Searsmont, Maine, owner Brian Totman works with his wife Susan and their three sons, Ryan, Matthew, and Joshua. A 30-year veteran of the towing industry — he's been doing recoveries since he was a teenager — Totman admits that it took him a little while to shrug off some of his "old school" methods. "I was an old-time tower — a sling and a truck, and that's it," he said. "Going from a sling to a wheel lift, it took me a long time to say, 'Yeah, I can do this.'"

One useful tool — the fifth wheel underlift — can make a big difference on the road. "We have them on all of our trucks," said Louis Anglin of General Automotive Services in Searcy, Ark. While Anglin notes that his drivers rarely use the fifth wheel underlift, it does come in handy in certain situations — for example, when recovering a tractor-trailer or while towing travel trailers.

"Typically we tow tractor-trailers in as a combo," explained Anglin. "About the only time we use the fifth wheel underlift is during emergency situations with a trailer, bringing it out of a parking lot or something like that."

If you're looking to save on costs, Kevin Hamman, owner of Hamman Engineering in Newbern, Tenn., recommends taking a look at the fifth wheel underlift. "To begin with, thepurchase priceof a 'fifth wheeler' is dramatically less than that of a wrecker body," said Hamman. "So from payments to fuel cost to maintenance, the cost of operationfor a fifth wheeler is much less than that of a wrecker."

According to Hamman, one big advantage of this newer equipment is that it improves the tower's quality of life. "At the end of the day," said Hamman, "he can accomplish more tows with less fatigueand lesschance of injury."

Airborne payment

What forms of payment do you accept from your customers? For many towers, the old-fashioned *ker-chunk* sound of the credit card slider has given way to fully electronic transactions. To bill customers, the Totmans use wireless technology: portable, wi-fi enabled credit card processing terminals. Slide the card through, punch in the price, and the transaction is automatically transmitted via satellite — no muss, no fuss.

"I charge up the machine overnight, then put it in the truck," added Brian Totman. The machine works "out in the middle of no-man's land where my cell phone doesn't reach. I just pull out my little machine and slide the card through, and I'm paid. You don't have to worry about carrying a traditional credit card machine, or making phone calls to authorize a payment, or coming all the way back to the shop to use the credit card machine." Before, said Totman, "It was, 'Do we take a check from this person, and if we do, will it be a good check?'"

This is a significant improvement in billing practices, especially in the rural areas that Totman Enterprises serves, where mobile phone coverage can be spotty. "The drivers don't need to call in, but can process on the road," explained Susan Totman. "There are a few spots with no access, but for the most part we're able to process almost anywhere within our area."

Bright lights

Because he works with his sons, Totman has a heightened personal interest in the safety of his employees and his towing equipment. "We need to be as safe as we can out there," he said. To that end, Totman's recent truck purchases have included LED lighting on the light bar, the carrier, "and all through the running lights and taillights," he said. Some of his trucks still feature strobe lighting, but Totman is gradually replacing that older equipment with LEDs.

"It's easier to see the LED lighting in the daylight as compared to strobes," continued Totman. "I bought one truck with LEDs, liked it, and that's how we started." According to parts manager Todd Suhr, LED lighting has been around for about a decade but has really taken over the marketplace in the last five or six years.

Installing LED lighting on tow trucks is a simple process, and Suhr sells a lot of the product to his customers. "With the strobe system you needed a power source and a cable to reach the strobe," said Suhr. "With the LED system you just need a power wire to the lights."

Equally useful are wireless towing lights that attach to the vehicle being towed. Butch Hogland, owner of Hooks Towing & Recovery Supplies in Wynne, Ark., said that wireless towing lights are one of his most popular sellers. "Customers have really used a lot of them," he said, "and they've been a major improvement from the old to the new."

Endless slings

What about slings? There's an updated version of that piece of equipment too. The Endless Round Sling is a flexible, lightweight alternative to the traditional heavy sling.

"It's a strap that's a continuous circle," explained Don Mesaros, owner of Auto Works Heavy in Milford, Ohio. The company performs light, medium and heavy-duty towing and recovery. "Continuous loops are useful because you can take one, go through the wheel, and you have an attach point." Lift, and there's no damage, said Mesaros.

When Mesaros first worked in the towing industry, "straps were expensive," he recalled. "When you're putting a strap on the bottom side of something to upright it, and you can't see anything, you might nick or tear it."

The straps are available in different lengths and provide more contact area across a surface than a chain does. "When you spread that load out, you're not nicking the side of the car or a panel," said Mesaros. "Let's say you want one for a car. You can buy a 4- or 6-foot sling if you're going through the wheel, or you can get an 8- or 10-footer if you want to wrap the car."

Mesaros praises continuous slings for their ease of use and

lightweight construction. A 10-foot chain, he said, weighs about 9 pounds per foot, while the endless sling weighs about 12 pounds total.

For heavier recoveries, Mesaros says he buys a lot of 20-foot slings, which work really well with airbags. "They stay in place because you've got a big grip on the surface," he explained. "I make protection sleeves to slide on the straps. And you don't have that chain going up the side of the trailer, nicking it all up."

Mesaros also says the price is right — gone are the days when he had to spend $1,000 on a sling. If a strap is nicked or breaks but doesn't do any damage to the vehicle, "the insurance company doesn't mind spending $150 for that strap because you've saved them $4,000 in damage," explained Mesaros.

Alloy snatch blocks

Finally, towers praise the use of metal alloys in snatch blocks. Tony Coffey, owner of Tri Power Towing in Effingham, Ill., notes that alloy pieces are, in general, stronger and lighter than their steel counterparts. "I have a 12-ton alloy snatch block that's lighter than my 8-ton steel snatch block," said Coffey. Gear made of metal alloys allows Coffey to boost his towing capacity.

Don Mesaros offers another weight comparison: "The old Johnson snatch block, made of steel, weighs 68 pounds," he said. "An alloy snatch block weighs 43 pounds. That's a whole lot of difference when you're carrying things up and down a hill."

"Really, anything made of alloy is good!" said Coffey.

Here's to continued improvement in towing and recovery equipment — providing tremendous benefits in safety, ease of use, and the tower's quality of life.

Voice of the Customer: Improving Towing Equipment

The towing business, on the manufacturing side, has often been a customer-driven process. After all, the creation of the first tow truck was the result of a customer need: *Get my vehicle out of this ditch, please!* Over the years, manufacturers have listened to customer input to produce new equipment that's needed on the road — and, of course, to stay in business in a very competitive marketplace.

What the customer says

Manufacturers note that their customers have had a huge impact on the design of new products. "Customer influence is essential for us," said Scott Rahner, product specialist for United Recovery Industries. Based in Kansas City, Mo., and Elizabeth City, N.C., United Recovery Industries manufactures tow truck and carrier bodies. "We are constantly in contact with our customers to improve and prototype equipment," added Rahner.

At Jerr-Dan in Hagerstown, Md., a continuous process called Voice of the Customer (VOC) provides helpful guidance for the company. "This input factors into all of our product development and product improvement programs," explained Jeff Barbour, director of marketing and channel management for Jerr-Dan. "Cost and ability to manufacture are key aspects of any project," added Barbour, "however, the demands of the customer who is using the product everyday are critical."

"We seek input from the end users including motor clubs and municipalities," said Anthony Gentile, president of Dynamic Towing Equipment & Manufacturing in Norfolk, Va. "Owning a towing company in New York helps us tremendously in testing changes made before [a product] hits the market," added Gentile. "Also it helps us understand how efficient and easy the unit needs to be out on the road."

Products formed by customer input

Steve Ford, engineering/technical director for Zacklift in Cle Elum, Wash., described a recent innovation driven by customers: "Towers have long been showing up at the scene only to find that wheel lifting is the best way to go. If only they could lift from the *outside* of the tires, bumping absolutely nothing on the chassis front end." At the same time, continued Ford, heavy-duty rigs are often put to the test when a smaller vehicle such as an SUV needs to be hauled.

Responding to this need, Zacklift updated its Heavy Duty Wheel Lift — now the number-one selling accessory for the company. "It does not require changing out any heavy cross bars or dragging on and off massive L-bars," explained Ford, who added that almost every Zacklift wheel lift is now outfitted this way.

On the opposite coast, Dynamic Towing came up with its own recent innovation, the slide-in unit. "It's for people who are looking for a low-cost unit to install on a pickup truck," explained Gentile. The slide-in unit has a 4,000-pound wheel lift, a 7,500-pound tow capacity, and bolts in with a standard electric-over-hydraulic pump or optional clutch pump.

Another Dynamic product that resulted from customer input was the Dyna Trac Rollback. The product was born out of many meetings with the AAA Club of New York. "We set out to build a unit that would do road service, battery sales and service, and towing — all in one unit," explained Gentile. The Dyna Trac Rollback uses two valve bodies, eliminating traditional linkages that can freeze in cold weather or wear out with heavy use.

Customer input is also paramount at Miller Industries in Ooltewah, Tenn,, where the Chevron, Vulcan and Century nameplates reside. John Hawkins, vice president of sales for Miller Industries, points to the company's new H-beam rotator as a good example of a product refined through customer input. When Miller kicked off the development of the H-beam, the company picked 10 operators who had been using Miller rotators for many years.

That focus group provided critical feedback during the design process for the H-beam rotator. "One of the things they absolutely demanded was that the underlift be an integral part of the machine," recalled Hawkins. "Some towers say that a big recovery vehicle doesn't need an underlift, but you can't sell a big rotator without one." Miller then showed seven design concepts to the focus group, which debated the advantages and disadvantages of each option.

Functionality, noted Hawkins, is a keyword at Miller Industries, so the focus group looked at the effectiveness of each design plan. "We took in excess of a year building this new machine, because it had to be right," said Hawkins.

Meanwhile, Jerr-Dan's Voice of the Customer product improvement process has contributed to a number of innovations at the company. The MPL self-loader line resulted from a lot of input from towers. The product line features negative tilt with level stop assist and a fifth-wheel/gooseneck attachment.

Additional Jerr-Dan products that resulted from customer feedback include the Side Recovery System, reconfigured controls and flip-down spade feet on Jerr-Dan's 16-ton units, improved storage options and tool management systems on heavies, and the new XLP-6 Low Profile Car Carrier.

Ron Nespor is director of carrier engineering for three of Miller's nameplates — Century, Vulcan and Chevron — manufactured in three plants in the U.S. Nespor considers his best design achievement to be Miller's LCG (Low Center of Gravity) Carrier, a product created partly via customer feedback. "The LCG carrier was a collaborative effort with Dave Jaeger of American Enterprise," said Nespor. "It incorporates a low-profile design that lowers the center of gravity of the carrier which improves handling, stability, load angle and payload height."

The lower carrier profile, continued Nespor,also makes it much easier to reach tie-down points for securing the vehicle loaded onto the bed. "And the lower load angle does a better job of loading vehicles with low clearance front ends," he said.

Finally, United Recovery Industries credits its customers with helping create the company's Universal Subframe. "The subframe almost doubles the original strength when it is used in our Classic Series units," explained Rahner, "while in the X-treme 2 units it provides a proven platform to build off of."

Soliciting customer input

Rather than waiting to receive phone calls and feedback forms, manufacturers actively reach out to their customers for information. Rahner says that customer input at United Recovery Industries is received on a constant basis through direct contact. "We speak to hundreds of customers a week about their current equipment, whether it's ours or someone else's," said Rahner.

On the sales side, distributors and salespeople provide information culled from their interactions with customers. "We maintain a marketing information depository," said Jerr-Dan's Barbour, "in which any information from customers, distributors or field sales force is entered. We can then identify and respond to recurring themes or ideas." For large projects, Barbour added, Jerr-Dan makes use of focus groups to refine the development process.

When customers contact a manufacturer, it's important for the company to make a good impression, notes Zacklift's Ford. "Zacklift's goal is to 'wow' them," explained Ford. "Listening to every customer, figuring out how to best meet their needs — this is the first step in communication."

Maintaining that relationship with customers, Gentile said, ensures that the company's product line will continue to serve the needs of the market. "We are constantly following up with customers," said Gentile. "We speak to them at tow shows. We also call them at times asking how everything is. We are always looking for input or ideas."

Hawkins notes that Miller studies products created by manufacturers outside of the towing industry. "We're always going to different trade shows," said Hawkins. "We don't get stuck within our industry." To that end, Miller sends representatives to trade shows that feature firefighting, marine and construction equipment, among others. This includes the triannual CONEXPO-CON/AGG international marketplace for the construction industries. "You want to see what people are doing outside your industry, and how to bring it into yours," explained Hawkins. As an example, he points to the composite boat bodies unveiled at marine shows: "We build a composite body for our wreckers. That came out of the boat industry," he said.

In the end, manufacturers understand the importance of communicating with their customers, and ensure that the communication works both ways. Steve Ford of Zacklift summarized his feelings about the importance of the customer in this way: "Every accessory that evolves, every change in mounting, standard equipment, valve layout, even color — is the result of having all eyes and ears open to what customers are needing. When focusing on customer needs comes first, then success naturally follows."

Chassis: Targeting the One You Want

You can't just plop some towing equipment on *any* chassis and call it a tow truck. It's not a marriage of convenience but one of form and function. A number of important factors contribute to the choices you make, and the chassis — the foundation of every tow truck — provides your starting point. Whether you go with Ford, Freightliner, GM, Jerr-Dan, Miller, or other brands of chassis on the market, selecting the right one for your business can make all the difference in the world.

Crafting the right truck requires careful coordination among a quartet of experts. "End-user, body builder, truck dealer and truck OEM [original equipment manufacturer] — those are the players," said John Hawkins, vice president of sales for Miller Industries in Ooltewah, Tenn. "For the most part — especially when you're dealing with medium- and heavy-duty trucks — each vehicle is customized for a specific towing or recovery application, so understanding how the vehicle will be used — and subsequently the spec'ing — is vital to success."

Going through the process

Jesse DeGraeve, owner of Anytime Towing in Traverse City, Mich., has purchased his share of new trucks over the years. DeGraeve picks the equipment and chassis by researching the specs of each, then meshing the information together carefully.

"When choosing a chassis, there are a lot of considerations," said DeGraeve. "But the first needs to be, 'What is it going to be used for?' The type of towing equipment being used on the truck is going to direct you to certain types of vehicles."

Once that decision has been made, said DeGraeve, the engine, power, and weight/GVWR [gross vehicle weight rating] need to be considered so that the chassis can support the towing equipment correctly. These considerations apply across the board, whether you're performing light-, medium-, or heavy-duty operations.

"It seems like after you look at those three items it narrows the chassis options down to three or four manufacturers," continued DeGraeve. Beyond that, the decision comes down to personal preferences regarding items such as cab configuration, what brands of engine are available, options in the cab, and visibility.

Climate is also important when choosing options for a new tow truck. "Here in Michigan," said DeGraeve, "our light-duty and medium-duty trucks are 4x4's" —an option that may not be needed in, say, southern climates, which tend to be warmer.

When discussing a new truck with a sales representative, "Most of them have the specs of the trucks pretty well laid out," said DeGraeve, "so you can choose what is best for you. I actually have only test driven one of my trucks before I bought it. It's hard to do, because the truck is going to be very different without any equipment on it."

How can a tower select the right chassis? List your preferences and then check availability, said DeGraeve. "My first truck was a Freightliner and I had very good luck with it. I now have four of them." DeGraeve is fortunate to have a Freightliner dealership nearby, so obtaining replacement parts and having the trucks repaired are fairly easy endeavors.

DeGraeve noted that his shop has also used chassis models such as Chevy and Dodge 5500s. "We also have a couple older Ford F-350s that have been good trucks," said DeGraeve. "We have reconditioned one of them so far and will be starting on the other one soon. It seems like that is sometimes a better way to go than buying new."

DeGraeve added that he put about $13,000 into redoing his light-duty wrecker, versus investing $60,000 to $70,000 to purchase a brand new model. "It took a lot of time and hard work [to refurbish the existing truck]," he explained, "but I'm not making a large payment every month."

Working together

As we mentioned above, DeGraeve is fortunate to have a Freightliner dealership nearby, so designing, purchasing and fixing his Freightliner trucks all go smoothly. To get an inside view of what happens at a dealership, we visited the Murphy-Hoffman Company (MHC) offices in Chattanooga, Tenn., where Sales Representative Charlie Hall has spent more than a dozen years helping towers create new vehicles.

"I work very closely with the Miller Industries towing and recovery equipment, their engineering people, as well as their distributors and naturally a lot of times with the end user," said Hall, who handles Kenworth chassis for everything in the Miller product line, from medium-duty carriers to 75-ton rotators. Hall also coordinates with Kenworth's engineering staff.

"There's a lot of forethought that goes into the chassis that [towers] put their unit onto," said Hall. While there is a catalog of standard chassis specifications for each towing application, towers often need to install additional gear for the jobs they do — and, sometimes, special add-ons as well.

"Most of the towers want big horsepower," explained Hall. "They want all the bells and whistles that you can put on one. Normally on our stock Miller chassis — medium-duty and Class 8 — we have full power windows and full power mirrors. We even put a sunroof in the truck. They're pretty well decked out," said Hall, and have "any creature comfort options normally available."

Additionally, said Hall, "Some people want leather seats, some people want cloth seats, some people want green widgets, some want purple widgets. Even though you have stock specs there are a lot of things that people want out there."

"I buy my Kenworth trucks from MHC Kenworth-Chattanooga so that I can have the tow bodies and rotators installed at the Miller Industries assembly plant in Chattanooga," said Bill Gratzianna of O'Hare Towing in Chicago. "But I still get great parts and service support from CIT-Kenworth here in Chicago and when I'm 500 miles from home and I need service on my Kenworth truck, I still get treated by other Kenworth dealers as though I bought the truck from them."

One new wrinkle that's important to mention: Federal truck emission laws that took effect recently are affecting how towers spec their new vehicles. "There are limitations on where components can go and what you can do," said Hall. "[The new laws] have limited fuel capacity and the style of exhaust that can be used."

Your favorite brand

Manufacturers hope that you'll love their products and purchase them again and again. This "brand loyalty" extends to tow truck chassis as well. For example, at Alpha Towing, Inc., of Marietta, Ga., owner Mike Patellis has purchased Jerr-Dan products in the past; today he is particularly fond of the Nissan UD cab and chassis. Why? "The UD will go 850,000 miles and about 15 years," explained Patellis.

Patellis also noted that the UD frame is constructed of tough steel, and the engine has an outstanding warranty. "The GVWR is perfect for towing cars and light trucks," he added. "The visibility for the driver is wonderful, and he sits up high over the engine." In addition, said Patellis, gas mileage is good: approximately 13 miles per gallon.

There are, however, some tradeoffs in staying true to a particular brand. Patellis said that the parts for the UD chassis cost a little more but are worth the money because they last longer. "Dealerships are rare to find and very expensive; however, the truck is worth the money for the long haul," explained Patellis.

Heading down the road

Patellis plans to stick with Nissan chassis for now. Looking to the future, he added, the weight of the vehicle being recovered is becoming more important. "With cars getting lighter in weight we will opt for the aluminum beds going forward," he explained. "It saves fuel, money and tires, as the bed is lighter. As far as chassis specs, Nissan has several lengths and GVWR to choose from."

In addition, Patellis made an important choice that affects all of his tow trucks: "We decided to tow everything on a flatbed," he said. "This helps eliminate damage claims."

Balancing wants and needs is crucial in designing new tow trucks for your business. "In our industry most folks want all the bling-bling they can get on their trucks," said Hall. "There's a lot of competition out there to have the biggest and the baddest and the meanest." But to create that top-of-the-line truck, added Hall, careful discussion and planning will always be crucial, no matter how advanced the equipment.

Can You Find Me Now?
Tracking Your Tow Trucks

Air traffic control — for tow truck companies? A computer that encourages you to drive more safely? That helps you avoid heavy traffic and reach your destination via the most efficient route? Sure. More and more towing companies are installing tracking systems in their fleets. Better yet, these systems can use GPS and everyday communications devices such as the smart phone you already have. Or, if you want to go upscale, you can install fancier items like mobile data terminals (MDTs) in your tow trucks

Tracking systems are in everyday use at companies such as Henry's Wrecker Service in Washington, D.C., which uses a fleet management system manufactured by TomTom Business Solutions of Concord, Mass.

"Our dispatchers are just like air traffic controllers now," said Fred Scheler, president and CEO of Henry's Wrecker Service. "With two 46-

inch flat-screen TVs in dispatch, we can very easily see the location of customers and drivers, so our dispatchers can assign the closest truck and give the customer an accurate estimate for arrival. By traveling fewer miles to each call, we have saved $40,000 per month in fuel costs and our drivers can get to more calls every day."

That's a heck of a sales pitch — but will this product work for you and your towing needs? Let's take a closer look at the burgeoning field of tracking systems built for the towing and recovery industry.

Tracking your trucks

Currently a variety of vendors supply tracking systems. These vendors include Beacon, FleetMatics, Ranger SST, Teletrac, Tow It Systems, towXchange, Tracker Management, Transportation Information Systems, and U.S. Fleet Tracking.

The ability to track the fleet is critical to running an efficient towing business, said Michael Geffroy, vice president of sales for TomTom. The 20-year-old company manufactures the WORKsmart fleet management system, which integrates tracking with navigation and dispatch capabilities.

"All towers want to know where their drivers are so they can send the closest truck to service their customers," explained Geffroy.

The beauty of a computerized tracking and navigation system is that it provides an at-a-glance, real-time visual of what's happening out on the road. "With a TomTom fleet management system," said Geffroy, "you can just look on the map to see which operator is the closest to the customer and send them clear instructions directly into the cab. The driver simply accepts the job and the navigator provides turn-by-turn directions during their journey."

Such systems can also save valuable hours during the workday. "You're not wasting time with wrong addresses," explained Geffroy, "so you can get to more customers every day." And, said Geffroy, tow truck drivers arrive at their destinations more quickly, which ensures a happy and loyal customer base.

TowXchange, based in Chattanooga, Tenn., offers the fleet tracking product BudgetGPS. According to Jeff Pesnell, vice president of towXchange, "BudgetGPS is primarily focused on the location of the fleet or vehicle but also includes features such as current vehicle location, vehicle location history (bread crumb trail), [and] notification of vehicles which are stopped." The product can also create reports for items such as driver distance, speeding and stops.

Not really speeding?

The ability to watch vehicle positions in real time "is helpful if you need to send a truck to a location, or you don't know where your tow trucks are," explained Todd Follmer, CEO of inthinc, a company based in Salt Lake City, Utah. "On the display we capture locations every 15 seconds and we send it to your desktop computer every minute. So, minute by minute, you know where all of your vehicles are."

Follmer cited an example: "We received notification that one of our clients was involved in a two- or three-car accident." Initially it looked like the client was at fault and would be on the hook for several thousand dollars' worth of damage. However, because of the tracking system installed in the client's truck, "we were able to go back and prove that the accident was not related to our customer's driving behavior," said Follmer.

The grateful client paid inthinc the ultimate compliment: The tracking system, said the client, saved the company — a small business — from having to close its doors.

Follmer also noted that the tracking system helps in cases where tow truck drivers are pulled over for driving too fast. "If the driver is unjustly accused of speeding, we have data that will exonerate him or her in those instances as well," said Follmer.

Changing driver behavior

Today's sophisticated fleet management systems also include the ability to track the driver's behavior on the road, said Geffroy. "For example, every time an operator speeds or harshly brakes or turns, he's costing the owner money, in maintenance, in fuel and in exposure. Everyone knows that bad operators wear out brakes four times faster than good operators.

And sooner or later, he's going to have an accident, and that's going to cost you money in repairs and raise your insurance rates."

According to Follmer, inthinc's tracking system shows, in general, that tow truck operators drive over the speed limit 20 to 40 percent of the time, and fail to wear their seatbelt 20 to 30 percent of the time. "There's also a high ratio of hard verticals and hard braking events that correspond to drivers going over the speed limit," said Follmer.

At inthinc, the primary focus of the products is on driver behavior. "So in real time you have a device that will coach your driver to be a better driver," explained Follmer. "We focus on those behaviors that are going to lead to accidents or lead to damage to the tow truck or to the tow vehicle."

Inthinc's system tracks specific driver actions, including the number-one cause of accidents: excessive speed. To encourage drivers to stay at or below the speed limit, inthinc's system uses an accelerometer to track the truck's movements on the road. Potentially dangerous movements include hard acceleration, hard turns and hard braking — all logged by the system.

In addition, the inthinc system looks for "hard verticals" — when a tow truck blasts through an intersection too quickly, or enters or leaves a parking lot too fast. Again, driver behaviors like these can damage the tow truck or the vehicle being towed.

Follmer points to an interesting statistic: per mile, the amount of damage done to tow trucks and tow vehicles is greater than the damage to any other commercial vehicles. "The insurance that tow operators pay is the highest among all vehicles operating on the highway," noted Follmer.

"The day we turn on the mentoring [system], we see an immediate change," said Follmer. Among the improvements noted were an increase in the wearing of seatbelts (up 10 percent) and a significant reduction in adverse driving incidents. "The change in behavior is cut and dry," noted Follmer. "There's not a lot of subjectivity to it, because you can see it in the data."

Another interesting statistic: By keeping drivers to the speed limit, fleets using inthinc's tracking system are seeing a 10 percent increase in miles per gallon. Drivers are using less fuel, saving money for the towing companies.

By setting speed caps and tracking this information, added Geffroy, towing companies can reduce the chances their operators will have accidents. The companies can then provide this data to their insurance companies to negotiate lower rates.

Latest advances

Portability is critical. Current tracking systems allow the towing company to track its fleet from any location with Internet access. "Our customers have used this feature to check on overnight crews before going to sleep," said Geffroy, "or logging in first thing in the morning to see if any on-call drivers responded to emergencies during the night so they could make any required staffing adjustments."

Jim Shellhaas, president of Ranger SST (Service Solutions Technology) in Cleveland, Ohio, describes their product as "an integrated dispatching, messaging, and GPS tracking and mapping solution." Shellhaas has an interesting perspective on the subject: "that the concept of 'tracking,' while great and helpful, is an idea that is already in the past."

Newer, more powerful systems combine the traditional GPS tracking function with mobile messaging — for example, call status, vehicle information and pricing — and integrate it with dispatching and business management (account pricing and invoicing, for example).

Jim Weaver, founder of Tracker Management Systems, Inc., encourages towers to think about integration, rather than standalone solutions, to obtain the best results. Weaver said that the biggest benefit of tracking a fleet with GPS and Mobile Data Terminals (MDTs) "is the total integration ofcallswith locations andtrucks with the location plusstatus of the vehicles closest to the call."

With "total integration," continued Weaver, "the desired benefits of this type of investment greatly improves, because now not only do you have fuel savings and history of what drivers are doing and when, but greatly enhanced dispatching capacity as well."

Collecting and processing the information

According to Shellhaas, a critical question for towing companies is whether the tracking application they're using integrates effectively with the rest of their business needs. A tracking system, said Shellhaas, should work seamlessly with a company's mapping, dispatching, mobile messaging, and business management functions. Without this, he believes that towing companies are simply purchasing various products that don't talk to each other — "buying a four-cylinder Chevy when they should be getting a turbo-charged Porsche at the same price."

At towXchange, the BudgetGPS tracking system integrates with the company's TOPS dispatch software in order to display pending call information as well as in-process calls being worked. "This integration offers tow company dispatchers a visual of the location of their vehicles as well as the location of pending tows and location/destination information of tows being worked," explained Pesnell. This, added Pesnell, allows for a more informed driver/truck assignment.

"In addition to BudgetGPS," said Pesnell, "towXchange integrates with many of the mainstream GPS fleet tracking providers. Features range from simple fleet tracking to included in-cab terminals to connected GPS mapping appliances with a full range of reports which are exportable and available for e-mail."

In addition to real-time tracking of their tow truck fleets, companies can also track vehicle traffic more effectively. TomTom's product "uses data on the traffic flow of millions of anonymous mobile phone users and connected TomTom devices to determine exactly where, in which direction and at what speed all these mobile phone users are traveling throughout the road network," said Geffroy.

With this system, continued Geffroy, the user receives detailed incident reports about the length and reason of the delays, the most accurate delay information, travel and arrival times, and alternative route proposals.

Getting used to it

How are drivers reacting to the installation of tracking systems in their trucks? After all, some of these systems watch the driver's performance closely — and we all know how much drivers resent being "nagged at," especially by a computer.

"There's a short adjustment period," noted Follmer. "The system basically coaches the driver in real time." What about drivers who are upset about receiving "report cards" on their road performance? "There's really no penalty," answered Follmer. "If you put your seatbelt on when it asks you to, and slow down when it asks you to slow down, you're fine."

The inthinc system scores every driver in the company's fleet. This allows towing company owners to focus their efforts on improving the performance of drivers who are generating the biggest risk to themselves and to the business, said Follmer. Again, "if the driver responds to the coaching, there is no penalty," he added.

Overall, said Follmer, response from customers has been very positive. "We have enterprises small and large where drivers respond very favorably," he noted. "In fact, they say that it really makes them more aware of how they're driving." In addition, said Follmer, tow truck drivers report that they are also driving their *personal* vehicles more carefully.

Tracking the future

Down the road, Pesnell predicts several new wrinkles in the world of tracking. "Connected GPS appliances (from vendors such as Garmin, TomTom, and the like) are fairly new," he said, "and you may see the addition of vehicle on-board cameras bundled with GPS products." In addition, said Pesnell, mapping is improving and he's seeing features such as integrated traffic and weather.

Shellhaas sees two key advances in the near future. The first is that towing operations will become more mobile — with "more diverse, more powerful, more robust, and more affordable devices."

Second, Shellhaas sees more "intelligent" dispatch in the future — for tow companies and motor clubs. For example, AAA "is assigning calls not based on a 'company-driven' algorithm (calling a specific towing company), but based on the availability of the right equipment (truck type) that is in closest proximity to a new service request (stranded motorist). The company operating the truck is a secondary consideration."

Parts: The Popular, the Most Useful, and the Ones You Should Know About

Time to check in with popular vendors and manufacturers and ask for their advice: What's new? What's popular? What's innovative? What should be hot but isn't well known just yet?

The answers are always interesting and sometimes quite enlightening. So let's go visit the parts department and find out what's up.

Jumper cables

Let's start with jumper cables — but not just *any* jumper cables. Nick Kemper, general manager of TowPartsNow.com, told us that PowerSafe jumper cables are one of the most important developments he's seen in awhile. "With all of the onboard computer components in vehicles today, some of the manufacturers are recommending that their vehicles not be jump-started, because a power surge can damage the components," Kemper told us.

According to Kemper, the PowerSafe Cables feature an in-line processor that regulates the current and prevents damage from occurring. "EnergySafe, the manufacturer, is offering systems with an Associated connector and with an Anderson connector, as well as standard clamp cables and a short adapter for portable jump boxes and chargers," added Kemper.

Winching it up

Moving to cables that *don't* carry electric current, Tabitha Pierce of Pierce Sales in Henrietta, Texas, points to winch cables as one of their most popular sellers. Because cable kinks and wears out over time, "use a cable tensioner and roller guide for your winch cable, and re-spool the cable once a week," said Pierce.

Butch Hogland of Hooks Towing & Recovery Supplies in Wynne, Ark., recommended an up-and-coming cable he calls "the Superman cable." The new All-Grip super swaged cable winch line cable has two primary advantages over conventional wire rope: higher break strength and better resistance against crushing. (*Swaging* is a process whereby a product is forced through a die in order to change its properties.)

The "Superman cable" is manufactured via rotary swaging, "which is a process of compaction," explained Hogland. "An oversized wire rope is swaged, which reduces the voids and produces a more solid cross-section of wire rope. The result is more steel within a given area, which increases the break strength dramatically." These characteristics also allow for greater outer surface area contact on drums and sheaves, added Hogland, which helps the cable resist being crushed or deformed.

"We have sold this [cable] to our customers with great results," said Hogland. One customer, located in Amarillo, Texas, used to replace his winch cable every six to eight weeks. After replacing his usual cable with the All-Grip version, "the cable has been on there for seven months and is still going strong," reported Hogland.

"That's very good for a driver who runs an average of 14 calls a day and most of the time works his days off," noted Hogland. "It's also great for the company to account for less down time."

100

Links in the chain

Some of the best-selling parts at B/A Products Co., in Columbia, Md., are chain assemblies, winch lines and wheel lift straps and ratchets. Vice President of Operations Fritz Dahlin noted that while the company sells parts, B/A ("Best Available") Products is, first and foremost, a manufacturer.

"All of our chain assemblies are welded in-house," explained Dahlin. "We have a large sewing department that sews everything from 1-inch cargo straps to 12-inch-wide trailer recovery straps." Dahlin added that the company swages winch cables of up to 5/8 of an inch in diameter.

Controlling the situation

Speaking of winch cables, one of the most popular offerings at Pierce Sales is the Lodar two-function remote control, which provides for wireless operation of a winch from up to 1,000 feet away. Because tow operators easily lose their transmitters out on the road, "consider using a Lodar 9811 LoCator," said Pierce. This device "reminds you to return your transmitter to the holder." This is a handy feature when you're busy clearing an accident scene, for example, and have more important things to focus on.

Another control system recommended by one of our popular parts vendors is the Mobile Control Systems Radio or Manual Pneumatic Controls. It's a product that's been around for a while and is "an outstanding innovation," said Kemper. The system "converts the control system on your truck to an air-pressure system," Kemper continued. "This eliminates worn-out cable controls and crossrod systems, and gives you the option of a radio-operated system so that you can operate the controls from anywhere around the truck."

Even better, said Kemper, these systems are not difficult to install, and you can purchase a system for your winch only — which is perfect for carriers.

Cradles and arms

Another recent innovation that Hogland recommended is the control arm skate. This item was developed "to aid the professional towing and recovery operator when encountering broken ball joints, twisted-off axles, sheared lug studs, and stolen wheels on cars, trucks and/or boat trailers and rental equipment," explained Hogland.

"There appears to be an increase in ball joint failures across North America from lack of maintenance and potholes due to the economy," Hogland continued. The control arm skate allows the tower utilizing a flatbed to relocate a disabled vehicle or trailer by using just one piece of equipment.

The Collins Manufacturing Corporation manufactures tow cradles and dolly cradles, and Nick Kemper recommends these products highly. "The tow cradle fits into a standard wheel lift 1-arm and cradles the vehicle suspension when there is no wheel," said Kemper. "The dolly cradle does the same on a tow dolly." Kemper noted that the use of these products helps prevent damage to both the towed vehicle and the tower's equipment. In addition, the towed vehicle will be more level during the tow.

Tried and true

We'll wrap up our tour of great parts by going back to basics: popular items that have been bestsellers for many years. "Our best-selling items remain the standard items that are on almost every tow truck: straps and ratchets," said Kemper. "Two-inch ratchets and two-inch lasso straps are our biggest sellers. Two-inch cluster straps, carrier winch cables, and carrier skates are right behind them."

At B/A Products, Fritz Dahlin lists the following as new and innovative parts that the company introduced to the towing and recovery industry: round slings, self-locking swivel hooks for winch cables, Cordura-wrapped recovery slings, and side recovery guides that protect your carrier's cable and side rails.

Meanwhile, twist locks manufactured by Pierce Sales "have been on the market for two decades," said Pierce. "Towers use them to secure sling arms and lengthen wheel lift arms. Pierce twist locks beat the competition because of their ease, simplicity and longevity," explained Pierce. "Weld them in place and go. They now come in a stainless steel and threaded option."

Dahlin also lists spill kits, trash cans, go jacks, and reflective vests among the items that the company has added to its line over the past few years — products that are always needed and will never go out of style.

Talking to the parts department

Creating a positive customer service experience can be a challenge for both the customer and the parts representative on the other end of the line. We talked to one vendor to get an idea of how the process works for their company — and how customers can get the most out of the people they buy from.

Before contacting your parts distributor, said Tabitha Pierce of Pierce Sales in Henrietta, Texas, try to collect as much information as possible about the item you need and the assembly on which you'll install it.

"To ensure you receive the correct part, we may ask for measurements, photos or detailed information about the part in question," said Pierce. The more you know about your tow truck and other equipment you use, the easier it'll be to order a part when you need it.

Also important, according to Pierce: be as patient as you can with the parts department. The customer service representative knows that you need the part as quickly as possible and should do his or her best to fill your order. The relationship between tow operators and parts suppliers is reciprocal. "We understand when our customers are down, business is down," said Pierce.

Finally, prepare for the unknown by having spare parts already on hand. "Stock the parts you use the most," said Pierce, to avoid last-minute emergencies. Overnight shipping can cost a lot of money.

The distribution network

While the parts supplier's goal is to get the part to the customer as soon as possible, this isn't always done in the same way. Some parts vendors warehouse a variety of products to ship, while others coordinate items located in different distributors' locations.

Fritz Dahlin noted that his company, B/A Products Co., in Columbia, Md., sells its products through distributors in the U.S., Canada, Mexico and Asia. Although B/A Products doesn't maintain its own call center with customer service representatives to interact with the customer, the company's distribution system affords it a wider network than the company could get on its own.

"While we would love to sell to individual tow companies," said Dahlin, "we believe the distributor system to be more efficient and reliable." By dealing with a local distributor, continued Dahlin, the customer gets the benefit of the distributor's knowledge of local equipment requirements and usage.

"For example," explained Dahlin, "California has different requirements for chain and winch lines than New York. In another example, if you are located in Oregon, and need a winch cable now, we can direct you to several distributors who stock them, saving you time and money."

Dahlin added that as a manufacturer B/A Products is able to run specials with no minimums and quick turnaround. "We have full test facilities to verify the quality of our products," said Dahlin, "and we ship 95 percent of our orders within 48 hours."

Whether you run a parts manufacturing firm or a towing company, growing your organization is important. Dahlin noted that B/A Products recently began stocking items from other manufacturers. This allows the company to offer its distributors "a complete line, one-stop shopping," said Dahlin.

Finally, Dahlin made a comment that's a good goal for all parts vendors: "If it can be used on a tow truck," he said, "we want to make it available to our distributors. Second, we have begun stocking a wide range of other manufacturers' products. We want to be able to offer our distributors a complete line, one-stop shopping."

The importance of rope

Butch Hogland of Hooks Towing & Recovery Supplies in Wynne, Ark., pointed to a new and very helpful item that towers should know about: the Supreem X-12 Rope Winchline. "This New winchline rope has eased its way into the market by surprise," said Hogland. "Its strength has gathered a lot of attention from the towing industry. According to Hogland, this brand of rope features a working load limit stronger than cable of the same size.

"Can you imagine dragging or hauling extensions, chains or cables down a embankment or across a field to pull a vehicle back," continued Hogland, "when [instead] you can throw this rope over your shoulder?" The answer is easy, said Hogland: "Work smarter, not harder!"

Hogland believes that the Supreem X-12 Rope Winchline will be "a big factor in the towing industry" for reasons including the following: "Extremely high strength, a working load limit that's better than cable, light weight, low stretch, floats on water, spliceable, provides more torque, safe handling, no razor edges, low recoil, no shrapnel" — at a weight that's one-ninth that of steel cable.

Lighting it up

There are new and unique lighting products being introduced almost every week, said Nick Kemper of TowPartsNow.com. A recent addition to the company's inventory is the MaximmaMWL Series of worklights.

Added Kemper, "Another interesting product that I recently received is the Road Strobe, a handheld, rechargeable emergency lighting device that can either stand on its base or hang from a traffic cone." This light features two sets of LED strobes — in a variety of colors — on one side, and another set on the other side. "While you're warning traffic with one side, you're illuminating a work scene with the other," said Kemper. "This one was developed by a tower, and we're helping to bring it to the marketplace."

Making a difference

When parts dealers hunt for new products to sell, what characteristics catch their eye? We asked Chuck Ceccarelli, owner of In the Ditch Towing Products, for his thoughts.

"We're interested in new, interesting, innovative parts that have come on the market in the last year or so," said Ceccarelli. "Everything from a special bolt to a device that helps with the job or improves the tow truck."

Ceccarelli added that his company recently completed final testing of a new product, the traveling Speed Chock. "Every year I hear the horror stories about a car coming off a carrier deck during the loading process because either the winch or wire rope failed," explained Ceccarelli. "There is nothing on the market to help prevent a vehicle from rolling off the deck."

Ceccarelli is also proud of the company's Speed Dolly. "We get phone calls and e-mails weekly from towers who say how much they love this product," he said. "They always say that they feel we really listened and got the design right for towers. It is very rewarding when you hear from someone who says your product is making a difference."

The Truth About Overtime

A number of years ago a dispatcher in Illinois filed a lawsuit against the towing company that had employed her for over a decade. The dispatcher's complaint? That the company had worked her anywhere between 85 and 116 hours a week — without paying her overtime. And when she crunched the numbers on her paycheck, the dispatcher realized that her overall salary was below the minimum wage.

Meanwhile, in St. Petersburg, Fla., the U.S. Marshals Service did some towing of its own, driving away a company's wreckers. After a jury decided that a former employee was owed $24,616 in unpaid overtime and other fees, the towing company failed to pay up. When the employee complained to the government, the Marshals stepped in.

These two court cases aren't the norm, of course, but they demonstrate what can happen when towing companies and their employees disagree about how payroll is handled. If you're paying your drivers on commission versus an hourly basis, how does overtime factor in, if at all?

It's a tricky process that depends on several factors including the geographical location of your company, the laws in your state and the amount of business that you do, says Jesse DeGraeve, owner of Anytime Towing in Traverse City, Mich. His company operates four tow trucks and two long-haul trucks in a city with a population of 50,000.

"Overtime is a necessity for us, especially in the busy season," said DeGraeve. Although he's careful to take good care of his employees, he stresses that the company owner also must keep an eye on the bottom line. When required, "I try to utilize part-time employees to cut down on the overtime, also cut hours and send people home early if there is nothing to be done," said DeGraeve.

Commission vs. hourly

Again, each towing company needs to decide on its own pay policy, based on a number of local factors. For some bosses that means sticking with a commission-based system. "I strongly believe in paying for results," said Gary Coe, owner of Speed's Towing in Portland, Ore., and former president of the Towing and Recovery Association of America. "So a commission pay program aligns the company goals with the employees' goals."

And what are those goals? "Getting paid for what you produce, allowing high performing employees to earn lots, and low performing employees to work at a pace comfortable for them," explained Coe. Therefore, Coe pays his tow truck drivers on commission, his auto technicians per billable hour, the town car drivers on commission, and tow truck salespeople on a percentage of the margin on each sale. Certain managers in the company receive bonuses based on the net profit of their specific operation.

In northern Michigan, DeGraeve uses a commission-based pay system for his long-haul trucks. It's a straight percentage, but it's also a different arrangement than the one he has with his hourly-based tow truck drivers. "In long-haul, the seasons don't fluctuate as much, and that seems to be an industry standard for trucking," said DeGraeve.

For towing companies that operate in a sparsely populated region like DeGraeve's, a commission-based pay system might not be the most sensible approach. "In this area [Michigan], we have two busy seasons each year," explained DeGraeve: "tourist season in the summer and snow season in the winter." Off-season is "pretty slow," he said. "If we used commission, it just wouldn't work out for the employees. I don't think I could keep good people if they were only getting half the pay in the slow season."

"I think that for a towing company that does more volume in a more populated area the commission thing might work," added DeGraeve. "But I would be afraid that customer service would suffer as a result of a driver trying to get as many calls as they can done every day."

Overtime math

Since the rules can vary from state to state, towers should check their local laws. For example, Coe notes that in his state (Indiana), "For every case we must calculate those commissions against the hours worked at minimum wage, plus overtime." Coe sets his employees' workweek at 40 hours. Overtime is triggered after 40 hours or whenever an employee works more than 10 hours in a single day.

At Avilla Motor Works in Avilla, Ind., "My drivers get an hourly wage plus 10 percent of the truck's gross," said owner Jeff Watson. "They punch a time clock, so anything over 40 hours is time and a half."

From the owner's perspective, it's important to do the math perfectly in order to ensure that employees are earning the minimum—and that less productive employees are given proper notice. "We must make certain that the earned commissions exceed the calculated minimum, or pay the minimum," said Coe. "Obviously we are not going to 'carry' someone who consistantly underperforms."

What about drivers who are "on call"? Because the employee must have the option of turning down an assignment, "having a backup driver on call is a must," explained Coe. If the employee has the option to turn down the call, then he is 'waiting to be engaged,' instead of 'engaged to be waiting,' where the employer must pay him or her for hours on call."

More options, different employees

If your towing company provides other services like vehicle repair, you have additional requirements to consider when deciding how to handle overtime issues. "It's auto tech where things get sticky," said Watson, who operates repair bays in addition to towing services at his Indiana business. "[The auto techs] are paid straight commission." The state requires that Watson provide his auto technicians with a base salary equivalent to the minimum wage or higher.

Therefore, the techs receive a guaranteed base of $300 per week whether or not there is any work to be done. "The other thing we do is make sure all our employees are on our workman's comp plan — even the part-time ones," said Watson.

On the other hand, when Watson needs to put technicians in a truck, he pays them the same commission as they would make in the shop, so they don't feel like they're being shorted. This complicates Watson's financial records and also dampens his bottom line. Moreover, any work in the shop has to wait until the call is completed. But it's also a necessity and the right thing to do, he says. "We try to keep the technicians in the shop, to keep both sides of our business flowing, but there are times when I just have to send them out, to keep up with the call, even if it costs me more."

Volume, volume, volume

DeGraeve said that the question of overtime is driven primarily by the volume of business he brings in. "One of my competitors here in town is a much larger operation and does a large volume with all the road clubs, which is the only way to make money with them," noted DeGraeve. When a towing company generates that much work, a commission-based system may work out quite well for the employee as well as the employer.

While he could have gone for volume in his company's business model, DeGraeve chose a different route. "I made the decision here to be a smaller company that provides good customer service, and that is what we focus on," explained DeGraeve. "When the phone rings, we know we are getting paid our normal rate, so when the driver is on overtime, we can still make money."

Motor clubs and overtime

How did DeGraeve arrive at this very important decision? After all, he could be making a lot more money if he had chased a volume business instead of specializing in single customers.

Previously about 20 percent of DeGraeve's business was attributed to road club members. "In my case I would say the clubs only paid us about 60 percent of what we would get from a normal cash call," explained DeGraeve. At the time, 90 percent of DeGraeve's night and weekend work was coming from the road clubs.

And here's where the need to pay overtime contributed to DeGraeve's overall decision to let go of his road club business. "After doing a lot of number crunching I found that, when the overtime was factored in, we were losing money or barely breaking even on most of these calls," said DeGraeve.

Though it was difficult to say goodbye to a significant portion of his business, DeGraeve says that the end result was best for his company. "We have been able to reduce our labor and overtime costs significantly," he explained. And, most importantly, "When our drivers are headed out at night or on weekends we are getting paid full price for what we do, not a negotiated or contracted price."

DeGraeve also says he was able to save on costs for maintenance and fuel. "I was also able to get rid of a truck (and its loan payment) and ultimately make my business more profitable," said DeGraeve — "not to mention easier to manage."

Education and Training
for Tow Truck Drivers

*Ever seen a tow truck driver in a Tuxedo? Well if you look closely, you won't
actually see them on our drivers either. (Our dry-cleaning bills were killing
us!) We live by our clean professional standards.*

This friendly opening paragraph on Alpha Towing's Web site not
only spotlights the company's insistence on well-dressed drivers but also
stresses owner Mike Patellis' focus on professional training for all of his
employees. Drivers at his Woodstock, Ga.-based firm must complete a
comprehensive 14-day training course that mixes classroom instruction
with hands-on experience.

While Patellis created his own training regimen, other towing
companies prefer to purchase their educational programs from a third
party. The towing and recovery industry doesn't have a single standard for

training and certification, but a number of organizations provide tools so that towing companies can ensure their employees are road-ready.

The market for education and training is big business, and for good reason: An estimated 35,000 towing businesses currently operate in the United States, according to the Towing and Recovery Association of America. And since each towing company has at least one employee, that's a lot of professionals who need to stay current on the skills needed to do the job—and for whom an official stamp of approval from a recognized educational agency is a seal of good business.

Like the rest of the towing industry, trainers have taken some hard knocks of late, said Terry Humelsine, senior lead instructor for Wreckmaster. "The current recession has had, to some degree, an effect on our industry in the training and education of their personnel." However, despite the recession's effects, Humelsine noted that "more and more municipal, state and federal governmental agencies—such as highway administrations controlling our nation's highways—are seeking and in some cases demanding trained and certified towing, transport and recovery operators for quick and effective highway clearance."

"With the emergence of sophisticated organizations with advanced in-depth training programs," Humelsine continued, "the towing industry at this time has produced and is continuing to produce some of this industry's brightest and most knowledgeable operators."

Training is available from various sources: companies such as Wreckmaster, The International Institute of Towing and Recovery, Miller Industries, North American Towing Academy, and others. The roster of well-known instructors includes names like Wes Wilburn, Tom Luciano and Terry Humelsine.

If you're looking to get certified, a number of organizations offer programs designed to meet that need. The Towing and Recovery Association of America, Inc., led by Executive Director Harriet Cooley and Cabinet President Alan Gregg, is based in Alexandria, Va. The nonprofit organization offers its National Driver Certification Program (NDCP), which was launched with a grant from the federal Department of Transportation.

The NDCP tests provide three distinct levels of certification. "TRAA has tested over 12,000 towers and participation continues to grow each

114

year," said Natasha Patterson, director of certification operations for TRAA.

According to Patterson, the TRAA Level 1 exam focuses on light-duty towing in five functional areas: customer service, safety, incident management, trucks and equipment. The Level 2 exam deals with medium-duty towing issues including professional service, forms and invoices, safe driving skills, customer and personal safety, specialized equipment, and recovery skills.

"Level 3 (heavy duty) testing is unlike Level 1 and 2," explained Patterson. "Testing is both written and an oral exam, and the heavy recovery specialist is tested on his or her analytical abilities based on years of experience rather than the strictly factual approach as in Levels 1 and 2."

TRAA testing is available nationally at local libraries, community colleges, national tow shows, and through certain state associations. Three years ago TRAA contracted with PSI Testing Centers to offer computer-based testing. TRAA also offers a variety of ancillary training DVDs that cover subjects such as dispatching, marketing, safety, and ANSI-approved apparel.

Training and certifying the driver

Bruce Pedigo, vice president of operations for Joe's Towing & Recovery in Bloomington, Ill., uses the TRAA certification tests to signify completion of the first phase of the company's training. "We start new drivers out with a minimum two-week training period," explained Pedigo. "They start out with a driver in one of our wheel lifts. For the first few days they just ride and do all the paperwork."

As part of their initial education, trainees familiarize themselves with company procedures and policies pertaining to hooking up vehicles, securing straps, dollies, go jacks, jump-starting vehicles, tire changes, and unlocking cars.

During this period the trainer also provides the new employee with hands-on experience—practical application of the information being taught. "We take the new hire out in the yard, roll a car over on its top and teach him or her how to roll it back over," said Pedigo. "This allows us to start thevery basics of recovery training as well as the proper use of the winches, snatch blocks and attachment points on vehicles."

After the first week the trainee moves to a flatbed and "starts all over, learning the procedures in loading and unloading a flatbed, the use of skates and motorcycle dollies," continued Pedigo. With the approval of the trainer, the new employee is then allowed to go solo, responding to certain types of calls.

Now comes the certification. At the six-month point Pedigo requires his drivers to have completed TRAA's level one certification test (for light-duty towing).

Follow-up courses

Once the new driver has been on the road for a year, Pedigo's company sends him or her to seminars sponsored by another popular training provider, Wreckmaster. "These classes help teach them some new tactics as well as reinforce the training we haveprovided them," explained Pedigo.

Wreckmaster sponsors a variety of training courses that have served over 23,000 towing operators since the company was founded in 1991. Nine standard levels of in-person courses — mixing classroom instruction with practical simulations — take students from entry-level basics in towing and recovery all the way to "exotic, unusual or loaded recoveries" and complex techniques. Students can be certified at each level.

Wreckmaster also offers a separate program for learning how to use air cushions to upright loaded units. There's also a week long seminar that teaches "the best tips and tricks of the trade."

In addition to teaching the expertise required for the job, courses like those provided by Wreckmaster have psychological advantages. "The biggest benefit to these classes is that they help adriver with confidence in his own abilities," said Pedigo. "We feel that utilizing hands-on training, combined with the TRAA testing and the Wreckmaster training courses, gives us very confident, qualified tow truck operators."

More educational options

Another educational entity, The International Institute of Towing and

Recovery (IITR), launched in 1988 as a non-profit organization formed by a diverse group of industry leaders, educators and trainers. Peter Fuerst, chairman of IITR, explained that the Institute was "originally known for its self-paced, self-study program that was delivered under the auspices of the University of Georgia Continuing Education Program."

Today, added Fuerst, "the programs now include an instructor-led Powerpoint presentation that includes a hands-on component."Current IITR course offerings include self-study and instructor-led programs in the operation of light-duty tow trucks, car carriers and road service equipment.

Since 2004 the IITR has operated under the umbrella of the Towing and Recovery Association of America Education Foundation, while at the same time remaining a completely independent educational entity. This is a good example of two towing organizations linking up to provide continuity in education: The IITR programs, said Fuerst, are a good way for tow operators to prepare for TRAA's National Driver Certification tests.

Scott Burrows, president of Burrows Wrecker Service in Pendleton, Ky., serves as a member-at-large for IITR. "New employees in the towing industry often arrive with sound mechanical knowledge, yet are painfully unaware of safe proceedures and operational requirements related to the recovery and towing of vehicles," Burrows explained. "The IITR methodology, outlined in their educational products, give step-by-step information in a systematic and logical manner."

Attending the academy

Based in Altamonte Springs, Fla., the North American Towing Academy is led by David Lambert, a 29-year veteran of the towing and recovery industry. Prior to founding NATA, Lambert created and taught training programs for the American Automobile Association and the Professional Wrecker Operators of Florida. He assisted in editing training programs for TRAA and IITR, and wrotethe AAA Towing and Service manual for nine years.

NATA provides two-day training programs in light-duty, light and medium-duty, and heavy-duty towing and recovery. The classes are both classroom and hands-on, followed by certification testing, valid for a five-year period.

Recently Lambert introduced a new one-day program for flatbed and car carrier operators. The course was built specifically for Towmasters (a New Hampshire-based non-profit chartered to provide education and training to towing professionals), but other associations have shown an interest in providing the class to their members as well.

"My business plan was to build the highest quality training programs available to the industry and offer them at affordable prices," said Lambert. "My heavy-duty instructor Garrett Paquette and I are working towers and certified instructors. We like to say we 'share' the information we've accumulated over nearly 60 years of experience between us."

Training the trainers, customizing the classes

Of course, training classes would be useless without skilled trainers leading the charge. To that end, organizations like the IITR work with towing associations across the country to ensure that trainers are prepared to teach. This is important, explained Fuerst, because otherwise the towing community could very well run out of trainers.

"The IITR is unique in that the IITR does not do training classes but develops the educational materials," said Fuerst. Once that's complete, the IITR "works with towing associations and auto clubs in developing their own instructors and training programs, using the IITR's nationally recognized curriculum."

As mentioned above, a number of educational entities cross-pollenate, assisting each other with training and certification programs. IITR helps prepare drivers for TRAA certification. And NATA offers special training programs that are designed to help members of state towing associations improve their scores on TRAA certification tests. "The program raised one association's test scores by 20 percent," noted Lambert. In addition, a NATA course for motor clubs focuses on improving customer satisfaction along with covering the standard towing and recovery curriculum.

Another way for towing companies to expand their training programs is to seek experience outside the industry. For example, Pedigo's drivers are cross-trained as certified flaggers so they can assist with traffic control at accident scenes when needed.

In addition, Pedigo's drivers learn about the job responsibilities of other professionals whom they meet on the road. "We train with our local fire departments so the drivers understand more about what the fire department needs from our company at an accident scene," said Pedigo. "We are always looking for improvements in efficiency as well as new techniques to tow and recover vehicles," added Pedigo. "So training never ends!"

State associations are involved too

Speaking of things on the state level, what happens after an organization like the Texas Towing & Storage Association decides to use a specific training program? "I certify drivers two ways," said Ken Ulmer, TTSA's education chairman. First, TTSA puts students through TRAA certification testing. Those drivers are then given a certification test approved in Texas and developedthru TTSA.

"As far as training goes," added Ulmer, "I and our esteemed TTSA trainers have trained thousands of drivers all over Texas and Oklahoma. We follow and base all of our training on the International Institute of Towing and Recovery (IITR)."

For training the heavy-duty arena, TTSA uses a course headed by internationally known instructor Tom Luciano of Miller Industries. Ulmer called this "the absolute pinnacle of training scenarios."

Lots of options

While our survey of education and training options is by no means complete, we hope we've given you a solid snapshot of the many options available to towing companies that are looking to upgrade their current employees' skill sets — or to initiate new drivers into the profession.

Regardless of how they build their programs, trainers and educational organizations all have one primary goal: to train and/or certify in the best ways possible. "Safety and professionalism are the primary purposes of the classes, but we also strive to instill confidence and pride in our students," said Lambert. "When we hand out those certificates and patches, both the students and instructors feel good about what has been accomplished."

Before the training starts

Before education and training begins for a new applicant, towing companies need to ensure that the person they're hiring meets some basic standards. At Alpha Towing in Woodstock, Ga., owner Mike Patellis looks for the following before kicking off any training for a prospective employee:

1. First, the applicant must pass a Department of Transportation drug test before an application form is provided. He or she must pay for the test as well. If the company hires the applicant, he or she will be credited for the cost of the test. This eliminates many applicants right off the bat.

In addition, said Patellis, "We do not hire smokers, as our property management does not allow smoking anywhere on our property, and we do not allow smoking in our trucks or office. Our clients do not want smokers on their property either."

2. A seven-year driving history must be submitted to get the application into the applicant's hands. This is required to be completed after the DOT drug test is passed.

3. As the application is completed, an interview time is scheduled. A few hours of tests are given to the applicant for reading, writing, math and map book skills, and towing knowledge. "We stress that work experience is mandatory in the towing industry," said Patellis.

4. If applicant is picked to be considered for hire, an I-9 form and criminal background check are done immediately. Then a DOT medical examination is completed.

5. Next, the driver is subjected to two intensive weeks of one-on-one training, followed by a safety ride with a sworn police officer. Several driving tests are issued before driver goes solo.

6. All of the federal and state paperwork, company rules handbook and required DOT forms are submitted.

7. The driver is assigned a unit and is on probation for 90 days.

Patellis notes that there are several reasons for this approach to hiring: "Those really looking for a job and are qualified we will consider hiring," he said. "Those looking for anything that pays until they can find another job generally don't apply. Many won't agree to a drug test and this ends all consideration immediately."

Unfortunately, added Patellis, many applicants will lie about experience, criminal history and health—and hope they never get caught. "We check as we go in our process," continued Patellis. "It has proven to work great for all concerned. This way we don›t hire the bad guys by mistake."

This careful, step-by-step procedure — including its check ride with local law enforcement — isn't all that surprising when you consider that in addition to being a tower, Patellis happens to be a part-time police officer.

What makes a great trainer?

What qualities are common to instructors who really know how to convey the material? We asked two well-known trainers, Tom Luciano of Miller Industries and Terry Humelsine of Wreckmaster, for their thoughts on the subject. Here's what they said:

"I believe the best trainers are people who have been in the towing and recovery field previously or even currently," said Tom Luciano, northeast regional sales manager for Miller Industries and a longtime instructor. "The best trainers talk from their heart. They previously have been engaged in the towing industry, so it's very easy to talk from the heart rather than just standing up and reading from a book."

"One other thing is 'never think you know everything.' When a student asks a question and you do not know the answer, write it down and tell them you will get back to them. Don't forget to keep your word. Get back to them with that answer, but be humble."

"The other thing that makes a great instructor is being able to relate to the tow truck issues at hand," continued Luciano. "Meaning, 'I've got this wrecker and it doesn't winch right. Do you have any ideas about where I can get information or ideas about how to fix this?' A great trainer can help answer that question or point them in the right direction."

121

"Part of being a great trainer is being mechanically inclined, because most of the people we talk to are not only truck drivers — they're mechanics and auto body people also. When operating a piece of towing equipment it is like having the specialty wrench to do a job — a crescent wrench does not correctly or professionally do it."

Terry Humelsine, senior lead instructor for Wreckmaster, said that "a truly great trainer or instructor is an individual who has given years of his or her life in the pursuit of excellence in the towing industry. They are individuals with a love and passion for our industry, coupled with the dedication to ensure that every student leaving a training class has been given and displays a level of understanding of the very latest in up-to-date research and development, as well as tested and proven methods, techniques and procedures in towing, transport and recovery."

Humelsine also noted that this list of instructor qualities represents the standards set out in WreckMaster's Instructor Training and Accreditation Program (ITAP). "They are simply individuals trying to raise the bar set by their forefathers for the operators of tomorrow to emulate," said Humelsine.

Computer Solutions in the Shop and on the Road

Whether you're dispatching by computer or charging customer's credit cards via a mobile device, chances are you're already utilizing — or are planning to adopt — some form of computer solution for your towing business. A number of vendors are dedicated to helping you do just that.

"[Our] objective is to work hand-in-hand with customers, enabling themto complete one more call per day per truck, using less fuel," explained Jim Shellhaas, president of Ranger SST in Cleveland, Ohio. "Towers are under a lot of pressure in today's economic environment."

A variety of useful software and hardware products on the market are assisting towing companies with their daily work. Beacon Software, headquartered in New Orleans, La., recently unveiled its TowLien.com online lien processing service. Among its features the service provides national registration searches, vehicle history reports, lien letters and static forms. TowLien.com can send documentation by certified or first-class mail. And a towing company employee can accomplish all of this on a desktop or laptop computer or on a mobile device such as an iPad.

What the software vendor needs to know first

For towing companies that are interested in installing new computer solutions or upgrading the technology that they already have in the shop, companies like Beacon, towXchange, Ranger SST and Tracker Management will need some initial information so they can offer suggestions to you.

At TowXchange, based in Chattanooga, Tenn., the company's first priority with its new customers is "to find out what they do and how they currently do it," said Vice President Jeff Pesnell. "Software should not completely change how you do your business but should improve the efficiency of your current processes while giving you additional information to use in managing your company." Pesnell notes that because of his company's large customer base, towXchange's software is flexible and can be set up to accommodate each customer's requirements.

Before contacting a computer solutions provider, make a list of what you think you need, recommends Jim Weaver, CEO of Tracker Management in Cleveland, Ohio. "If a company first looks at what they need to improve the running of their business and make a list of those items, it is much more likely they will get what they need," said Weaver.

Weaver also noted that towers must understand, to the best of their ability, the technology they are buying (or renting). He estimates that well over 50 percent of tow business owners are very uncomfortable with the technology of a management system.

"Most every software company out there will try to sell you on what they have to offer," continued Weaver. "And because many times the talk is what we call 'technobabble,' the focus ends up on the wrong subject."

The size of the towing company often drives the scope of the computer solutions it purchases. In a nod to his competitors, Weaver noted this: "At Tracker, I have found after 20-some years, that we have the ability to better understand all the complexity of all the different sizes [of] business. We know Tracker is not the best solution for all companies, and we are perfectly okay with helping a business owner sort out what they really need and make suggestions."

What's available?

Vendors offer a wide range of products that can be tailored to your company's needs. Shellhaas, for example, said that his company's product integrates a variety of features into one system. Those features include dispatching, GPS tracking/mapping, mobile messaging, impound/ storage lot management, stand-alone revenue accounting and invoicing.

As for individual functions, here are a few examples from the vendors:

Dispatch. According to Pesnell, towXchange's "TOPS, TOPScma, TOPSpd, TOPSlink, TOPSmobile and TOPSweb are all very strong dispatch offerings and implemented in various ways to serve towers and the customers they serve." How useful are these products? Pesnell said that over the years his company's software has dispatched over 18 million tows.

Maintenance. Weaver said that Tracker Management offers two types of maintenance tracking in its products, including what Weaver touts as the most advanced Job Cost module in the industry. "All the company has to do is to post expenses and allocate them to the proper truck, and Tracker takes care of the rest and then gives the owner a detailed breakdown for the month for each truck," said Weaver. The breakdown shows the cost of running the truck for the month, to include profit per call, profit per mile, cost per mile, profit per mile, and average miles per call.

Accounting. "We have the only tow management software that we know of that actually has a totally builtA/R (accounts receivables) and A/P (accounts payable)," said Weaver. "So there is no need for add-on software such as QuickBooks [a popular accounting software for businesses]." But Weaver also noted if a client already uses accounting software such as QuickBooks or Peachtree, Tracker can integrate its products with those software suites.

Don't forget the hardware

If you don't already have computer equipment on which to install your new software, most vendors will figure it out for you. Your most important consideration is whether you require desktop or portable computers — or a mix of both.

For the customer's convenience, Ranger SST can bundle its software with an assortment of hardware. "Our software is web-based and therefore accessible from anywhere the customer has an Internet connection," explained Shellhaas. For hardware, Ranger provides a wide range of integrated GPS/mobile messaging options "spanning device types, price points, and networks."

Among the hardware devices that Ranger offers are the following: mobile data terminals, Verizon Netbook computers, HP Slate tablets, Garmin Fleet Management units, PDAs/Blackberries, and Nextel ruggedized phones.

Going even more mobile

Computer solutions companies are always racing to develop fresh products to use with new technology in the marketplace. For example, Weaver noted that "Tracker Touch" — touch-screen software that combines the mapping aspect of GPS units with a visual of actual calls on a map — is a new product that "takes modern dispatch out of the dark."

"With Tracker Touch, towers can locate and assign the closest available truck to a call within a few seconds," explained Weaver. Because the system uses a touch screen, neither a mouse nor a keyboard is required. Also, the software "makes it easy for anyone to dispatch without the need of really knowing the streets of their city," said Weaver.

Shellhaas said future developments in the industry won't focus on software. Instead, hardware will be most important. "The mega trend is *mobile*," he explained.

"Think about your phone," Shellhaas continued. "It wasn't that long ago (circa 2005) when a Motorola RAZR (the successor to the StarTAC) was pretty cool. There are now more smart phones in use (over 75 million) than conventional cell phones.

Five years ago, said Shellhaas, state-of-the-art towing technology included separate pagers, GPS devices, PTT (push-to-talk) phones, radios, and credit card swipe devices. But the use of all these different technologies, mixed together in a potentially confusing stew of hardware and software, are actually an impediment to expanding a company's use of computers.

"Many companies feel stuck because they invested in stand-alone, single-purpose mobile technologies [as opposed to] an integrated solution," said Shellhaas.

Pesnell agrees, noting that future handheld technology offered by towXchange "will change the way auto pounds operate." Also, said Pesnell, image storage on the call record (photos or scans of documents) is a very popular recent addition to the marketplace. "It may very well give towers the ability to be paperless as soon as current laws are changed to allow this," said Pesnell.

Finally, Todd Althouse, president of Beacon Software, also had some thoughts on the future of mobile. "We will be focusing hard on mobile solutions such as smart phones and tablets," said Althouse. "We will have several product add-ons to our current line that will support most smart phones and tablets. The products will be targeted at the smaller owner/driver companies as well as the larger towing companies."

Beacon is testing its new offerings by late summer this year for release in the near future. Althouse added that these products will support credit cards, GPS and other Bluetooth features — all from a mobile hand-held device.

A fun job

With so many challenges ahead for computer solutions providers, we were curious about why they decided to get into this particular business — and why they enjoy working with towers every day.

According to Shellhaas of Ranger SST, "Helping our customers take their game to the next level of operational performance and become the recognized leaders in their markets is tremendously satisfying for the Ranger team."

"From a commercial perspective," continued Shellhaas, "it is a genuine win-win: customers essentially cover the costs of the Ranger solution on the first day of each month, and grow their profits for the rest of the month."

According to Weaver, "Tracker was founded on the principles of 'find a need and fill it' and 'if you help enough people get what *they* want, you get what *you* want.'" Weaver refrained from using the words *computer* or *software* in his company's name. "I never felt we were those but rather more of a total solution for office needs," he explained.

"I get my enjoyment out of helping companies go from good to great," Weaver continued. Two of his customers, for example, have grown from six to over 50 trucks each. "They have told me they could not have done it without Tracker," said Weaver. "Now that makes my day!"

"Our products help towers have a better quality of life," said Pesnell of towXchange. "It's easy to sell something you believe will help towers as much as our products do."

The Top 5

Jim Shellhaas of Ranger SST lists five key operational objectives common to his customers in the towing and recovery industry:

- **Getting dispatchers off of the radio**: electronically exchanging call data (not SMS or e-mails) with a mobile messaging solution in the truck.

- **Minimizing truck "drive time" to an incident**: having a navigation device (e.g., a Garmin) inside the truck is the easy part, said Shellhaas. The hard part is in obtaining and verifying correct incident/destination addresses — latitude/longitude coordinates — and forwarding these to the mobile device.

- **Equipping dispatchers to make better operating decisions**: providing mapping tools that show dispatchers the best options for assigning a truck to a new call.

- **Enabling drivers to electronically clear calls**: sending account-specific parameters so that the mobile device can calculate the right price for a call, and then process the credit card. The dispatcher can then have the next call display on the mobile device, so the driver can head over to his or her next destination.

- **Monitoring the "pulse" of field operations**: dispatchers need real-time information on whether mobile devices are communicating as expected, and whether the driver is wasting fuel, *before* it is wasted (for example, speeding or waiting for an assignment while running the engine).

Best Defense: Legal Protection in the Shop and on the Road

It's been a long day. Multiple calls come in. Your winch line wears out while you're performing a recovery. A customer unloads his frustrations on you. Some kids break into your storage yard and steal parts off a customer's car. While releasing a vehicle back to a customer, you notice some damage that you didn't see before.

If you're held liable for an unplanned incident that occurs in your shop or while you're out on the road, things can get quite sticky.

But since — to paraphrase a classic quote —the best offense is a good defense, there are a number of ways you can protect yourself from possible legal action. And if the worst should happen, rest assured that you've done your best to prepare for what's in store.

Protect yourself with education

Training: not only does it prepare you to do the job, but it can also prepare you to deal with unplanned incidents that occur while you're *doing* the job.

"Training. The biggest thing is training," agreed Ken Kallmeyer, owner of Ken's Crescent Springs Service, LLC, in Crescent Springs, Ky. "Keep your eyes open and try to avoid problems. Things are going to happen, but you can try to minimize them by making sure you have the right training."

"All towers should avail themselves of training courses through Tom Luciano, Wreckmaster, Wes Wilburn or other recognized leaders in the industry," urged Peter O'Connell, an attorney based in Albany, N.Y.

Kallmeyer recommends that towing companies ensure their employees are given plenty of safety training. "That's the biggest piece of advice I can give anybody," he said.

Getting that insurance

Also important: obtain the right type and amount of insurance from a good insurance agent. "Don't got at it half-cocked and get partial insurance on what you need covered," urged Kallmeyer. "Find a really knowledgeable insurance agent who has been involved in the towing business for a long time."

Morey Daniel is an insurance agent for Zurich North America, the second-largest writer of commercial general liability insurance in the U.S. Most states, said Daniel, will require that you obtain a DOT (Department of Transportation) number and at least $1 million in liability insurance.

There is, of course, a mix-and-match option when it comes to setting up an insurance policy. "There are different ways to combine limits," said Daniel. You can have lower limits but you can also buy "umbrella liability insurance" that provides additional protection. Daniel noted that he handles towers' insurance policies worth $1 million "up to probably $10 million."

Any type of general liability claim will fall under those limits, continued Daniel — "any type of injury that could occur to a person or people, any injury or damage that you might do to another party. You're covered if you have a load fly off your truck, if you hit somebody in one of your trucks while you're on your way to an accident scene, those kinds of things."

Prevention

In addition to having the right kind of insurance, "Prevention is always the best protection," said attorney O'Connell.

Some of the items on O'Connell's checklist: "Inspect equipment daily in order to determine that it is in good working condition. Injuries [occurring] to a customer riding in a truck is always a mixed bag.

"Of course," added O'Connell, "the customer wouldn't be injured if he or she wasn't riding in the truck in the first place. On the other hand, there could be increased liability if you leave a customer on a busy highway or under other circumstances that could lead to injury or death."

Also, said O'Connell, "you should never allow a customer to ride in a towed vehicle or in a vehicle that is on the back of a flatbed." Risky activity can trigger problems with your insurance company — or, worse, the outright cancellation of your policy.

Another way to limit your personal liability, according to O'Connell, is to incorporate or form a limited liability company (LLC).

Things that can happen in the shop

If you offer additional services to customers beyond towing and recovery, you'll need additional insurance. Towers who also run a garage and perform repairs on vehicles need to have operations coverage, Daniel said. "Generally the limits for operations coverage will match the limits for your general liability insurance." However, some insurance companies will offer different limits for liability and operations coverage.

But here's a catch for towers who also do repairs: your insurance may not cover you throughout the entire process of towing, repairing and releasing a vehicle to a customer.

According to Daniel, most insurance companies offer coverage that's effective only after the repairs have been completed, the customer has taken possession of the vehicle and has left the premises. If anything happens to the vehicle while it's in your possession — for example, something breaks while your mechanics are repairing the vehicle, or the vehicle dies during a test drive — "at that point in most places there is no coverage," said Daniel.

To avoid this issue, said Daniel, ensure that you have coverage for vehicles while they are in your possession — in addition to coverage for what may occur after the customer picks up the vehicle.

O'Connell agrees. "A towed vehicle is not covered under a general liability policy. Special 'on hook' or garage keeper's legal liability [insurance] is necessary," said O'Connell.

"Any time you can get both ends of it covered," explained Daniel, "you're always better off."

What is the "Prudent Man/Woman Rule"?

Potential lawsuits are a scary proposition for any tower, especially these days. "We have become a litigation-hungry society with lawsuits arising from seemingly silly incidents such as spilled hot coffee, air turbulence, etc.," said Travis Barlow, owner of the Travis Barlow Company.

Barlow and his staff have provided insurance for tow trucks and auto transport businesses throughout the U.S. since 1983. The company's offices are located in Pooler, Ga., near the city of Savannah. "We're the largest insurance agency providing insurance directly to the industry," noted Barlow.

How can you, as a tower, mitigate your exposure to possible lawsuits? By remembering the "prudent man/woman rule," said Barlow.

This rule, based in English common law, says that you should conduct yourself and your business in a manner that a normal person would, given the circumstances. Failure to do so is considered "negligence" and you would be liable for damages to an injured party for your failure to be "prudent."

"If you agree that a 'prudent' tow truck owner would not permit a convicted drunk driver to operate a tow truck," explained Barlow, "then you understand the rule. Who in their right mind would keep a drunk driver operating a tow truck? It would not be prudent."

Barlow continued: "Federal and state law says you should be prudent in selecting your drivers and that you must review their driving records at least once a year and be 'prudent' in evaluating their suitability to drive a tow truck. Insurance underwriters are very concerned that their insured's be prudent and obey the law."

Failure to be "prudent" exposes the insured to a potential lawsuit if someone is injured, warned Barlow.

Doing the job carefully

O'Connell reminds towers that there are other potential liabilities beyond injury to a customer. For example, "OSHA [the Occupational Safety and Health Administration] can nail a tower with huge fines for maintaining defective equipment, either on the road or in the shop." In addition, OSHA also can fine a towing company if employees aren't wearing proper high-visibility protective clothing.

You can't plan for every possibility, and you can't avoid every accident. But recognizing this can go a long way toward protecting yourself in the best ways possible.

Kallmeyer's best advice for keeping out of trouble? "Be honest with yourself and be honest with your customers. Don't be a rip-off, and don't do it for nothing."

No matter how well you train your employees or how carefully you hook up a disabled vehicle, bad things can still happen. "Something's always going to happen no matter what you do and no matter how well you plan for it," said Kallmeyer. "Sometimes you're going to get the bear, and sometimes the bear is going to get you."

Recognizing this — and rolling with the punches as best you can — will help your business continue to move ahead, no matter how many unfortunate things happen along the way.

Being prudent

Travis Barlow, who has provided insurance coverage to towers for more than 25 years, encourages towers to remember the "prudent" rule of law as they go about their daily work.

"You can help yourself by understanding this 'prudent' rule of law and being very diligent in the way you run your business," explained Barlow. Sometimes, however, the other party may decide to come after you in court. Here are some notes for towers regarding potential lawsuits:

- Know what the law requires of you.

- Be "prudent" in the way you run your business so you will be "defendable" if someone sues you.

- Help the insurance company defend you by being as "prudent" as possible.

- [If you have to go to court], ultimately a jury will decide if you have been "prudent" and will decide how much, if any, money should be awarded to a plaintiff suing you for negligence.

- Think as "prudently" as possible at all times in the operation of your business. Help the insurance company help you.

Working Smarter, Leading More Effectively: Better Business Management for the Tower

You need more than good old-fashioned business sense to run a towing company. These days, being old-fashioned may actually help run your company into the ground. Time to check in with a group of experts to see how towers can lead their companies in a 21st Century business landscape that constantly throws new challenges at owners and employees alike.

Elements of good business management

Where to start? First and foremost, build a solid foundation to your business. "Define why you are in business," said Rudy Smith of Rudy Smith Service, Inc., in New Orleans, La. "Spend the time to create written goals and objectives. Formulate a written business plan that allows you to achieve those goals and objectives."

After that's done, continued Smith, towers should create written company policies and procedures. This is the "road map" for achieving your goals and success, he explained. "The word 'profit' has to be in those goals, and the definition of the word profit has to be clear in your mind. Write it down and review it often!"

However, the road map is useless unless the towing company has a strong boss leading the way. "The most important role of any business owner is that of leadership (which is different from management)," said Stacey Tucker, owner of Chico Towing in Bremerton, Wash. Your ability to create a vision for your organization — and inspire your team to fulfill that vision by constantly communicating it to them — is critical, she said.

Being a leader, Tucker continued, means having the ability to work through crisis situations and turn them into opportunities that enhance your business. "Being a leader also means that you need to have a good understanding of what your strengths and weaknesses are, and that you must be willing to take on challenges that help you to grow personally," said Tucker.

"A leader will make sure that his or her support team has complementary assets, so that the team as a whole will be stronger than the individual pieces," noted Tucker. "No football team every won the Super Bowl with only quarterbacks."

Your people

The people whom you lead must be good at what they do — don't settle for second best. "Hiring quality people is key," said Coe. "They are representing you in the marketplace. Make sure they project your desired image."

When Tucker hires new employees — regardless of position — she lets them know that if she fails to provide them with the training, education and tools to perform their jobs adequately, it's her fault, not theirs. On the other hand, "If I've provided them with that and they are unable to do the job," said Tucker, "then I expect them to take responsibility."

Having a written and hands-on training program, along with company policies and procedures, is very important, continued Tucker. "Additionally, to be successful in business, I believe it is critical to have ongoing training and refresher courses as needed."

To ensure that you're guiding your employees in the right direction, consider putting together a team of advisors whom you trust. "It is very difficult, especially in a small business setting, to be all things to all people," said Tucker. She recommends that towers pick their advisors from various career fields, including accounting, banking, insurance, industry colleagues and other small business owners.

However, do not use employees, family members or other people in the industry, said Smith. "The idea is to expand your network and get a different prospective from business people who do not share your experiences and opinions."

Smith recommends that towers meet with their advisory board at least six times a year to discuss business opportunities and problems. "An advisor group can help you find prospective and knock you back into reality when you get sidetracked," said Smith.

Money matters

Your pockets may not be very deep at times, but careful tracking of your budget can help you weather economic storms such as the one that's been battering local business across the nation for the past several years.

"Understand your costs," urges Dennis Wencel, a towman and author of *The Black Book of Towing*. "Understanding your total cost per call is an empowering position, but I believe few towers want to go through the hassle of calculating this number." Wencel labels this as the "Magic Number."

"There are some instances when you may want to perform a tow for less than your Magic Number," explained Wencel, "but it is always nice to know when you making that decision." If you don't know that number, he added, you'll be unaware of when you're losing money on a call.

Gary Coe of Tow Consulting, LLC, recommends that company owners keep their total labor costs well below 50 percent of revenue. This should include the owner's salary. Although you may be tempted to leave yourself off the payroll, "make sure you take a salary," said Coe.

If you are not currently using a good software program for tracking your expenditures, Tucker recommends that you seek assistance from an accountant. This will make sure that you are getting all of your financial information properly recorded and that you review it in a timely manner.

"Produce financial statements as early as possible each month, added Coe. "Learn to understand them. Modify them so that they are most meaningful to you." Profit and Loss statements are critical, said Tucker. "Analyze [them] to be sure that you are recognizing trends before they become a problem."Balance sheets can help your financial institution track debt ratios and monitor the overall health of your business.

Getting the word out

After your business and daily routine are established, it's very easy to start operating in a vacuum. Unfortunately, this can mean that your company fails to grow its customer base from year to year. You can reverse this trend by breaking out of the box in which you're operating.

"Ask for the business," said Coe. "Don't wait for someone to call. If you are too shy or too busy, hire someone, full time or part time, and pay them on results. You must ask for the business."

Smith agrees. "Expand your contact network," he said. "The average person knows 2,000 people. My contact manager contains over 4,500 people. Each one of those people knows my name and, more importantly, knows 2,000 other people. That is nine million contacts with only one degree of separation."

Smith also recommends that towing company owners get involved with owners of other types of businesses. "Join an executives' association or the chamber of commerce," he said.

Give technology a big hug

If you're not already investing in the latest technology for your towing business, it's time to reconsider. "Embrace technology and other systems to help you manage," said Wencel. "So much of running a towing company is efficiently maintaining the routine. Employing technology like dispatching software to assist during the call spikes, or even something as simple as a company form to track preventative maintenance schedules for the equipment, can really help managers manage more effectively."

Computer software that helps with management, tracking and accounting "are more valuable than your tow trucks, in terms of reaching goals and achieving profits," said Smith.

When it comes to connecting with your customers, the ubiquitous smart phone can be your best friend. "Maintain a nimble and evolving online marketing plan," recommended Wencel. "Simply put, the most scalable source of high-profit work for a tow company is cash call work. Over 70 percent of Americans own smart phones." The battle over who gets these calls, said Wencel, will be won by companies prepared to communicate effectively with prospects who use their smart phones to find a towing company.

Management challenges of today and tomorrow

What are the biggest challenges that industry leaders will face in the coming years? One critical issue, said Coe, is in dealing with motor clubs. "We must find a way to deal with the auto clubs, who have become the middleman, and absorbing all of the profits," said Coe.

Coe's second big issue is with overregulation by state legislatures and city councils. "And that is not just towing," he explained. "That is business in general. Take the handcuffs of business! You can tell I'm a whole lot passionate about that subject," said Coe.

Wencel points to employee healthcare costs and online marketing as two key issues facing towers now and in the future. "Tow companies still alive after this recession will have learned how to do more with less," he said. "These survivors will know how to operate efficiently and most should be in a good growth position when demand returns."

Meanwhile, said Wencel, Internet search companies are heavily focused on improving local businesses' search results. "Over 50 percent of Internet searches include some form of geographic qualifier, so learning how to make sure your business is showing up in your customer's searches in the key to securing your share on calls sourced from an online search."

Company managers, continued Wencel, also have to be willing to incorporate social marketing into their businesses by asking satisfied customers for online reviews, maintaining a company presence with social media tools like Facebook and Twitter, and by understanding the value of positive online customer reviews — and the cost of negative ones.

It's a lot to take in, but the savvy tower has a better chance of surviving in an increasingly complex and competitive marketplace. "If you are not changing, you are not improving," said Smith. "Accept that change is necessary in order to improve and build a successful, profitable business."

TRAPS TO AVOID by Stacey Tucker

Stacey Tucker, owner of Chico Towing in Bremerton, Wash.:

1. *Micromanagement.* Train your people to "think like the owner."Not only will micromanaging everything burn you out, your employees will also really resent it.If you have faith in whom you have hired, you need to support them by allowing them some leeway to make mistakes. Yes, mistakes will be made, but if you give employees both the responsibility *and* the authority, both sides will end up winning more than losing.

2. *Not understanding your role as a business owner.* Many of today's owners in the towing industry started out on the ground level as drivers and likely had a great deal of success in that arena. While technical knowledge is invaluable, sometimes it doesn't translate into running an effective business. If a business owner finds himself or herself in the position of "driving the desk" and doesn't have the skill set to excel, it may be time to go back to school and take advantage of training and workshops that will provide specific skills to implement in the business.

3. *Burnout.* One of the greatest traps in our industry is the fact that the business is 24 hours a day, seven days a week. Many of us in the industry eat, breathe and sleep towing. This is not necessarily the healthiest option for a business owner, and it creates a perfect opportunity for burnout. Everyone needs to get away from the business, plan a vacation (*not* attending a tow show!) and let your mind rest and rejuvenate. Of course, this is easier said than done, but without taking time away you will not realize the benefit of a rested mind and the ability to come back to your

business with fresh and new ideas. Leave your business in the hands of a trusted employee. He or she will do fine!

4. *Not participating in activities outside your business.* I believe that it is very important to stay active in your local/state association. This provides you with the opportunity to interact with other professionals, receive good industry information, and learn from mistakes that others have encountered. Additionally, it is always useful to make sure that you are participating in your own local community. Not only will this give you perspective on what's going on there, but it will also help the people in your community put a face to your business. Remember, people do business with other people.

TRAPS TO AVOID by Dennis Wencel

Dennis Wencel, towman and author of *The Black Book of Towing*:

I think the biggest trap towers fall into is getting isolated from the rest of the world. Running a tow company will consume your every waking minute if you allow it to.

It's important to both maintain contact with the greater towing community as well as the greater business community so you have access to innovative business ideas to keep your company current and competitive.

The former can be accomplished by attending tow shows, joining your state association and reading the many Internet blogs dedicated to the industry. The former can be accomplished by joining and participating in events hosted by your local chamber of commerce or by joining organizations such as Rotary International.

The biggest trap I was guilty of falling into as an owner was in getting too comfortable with employees who were "just okay." It was sometimes easier to overlook and not address employee shortcomings because I didn't want to deal with them or because I knew the solution would ultimately be replacing the employee — which represented a headache I wanted to delay for as long as possible. Finding quality employees in our industry is a challenging task. Looking back, I can see that I often settled for "okay."

TRAPS TO AVOID by Rudy Smith

Rudy Smith of Rudy Smith Service, Inc., in New Orleans, La.:

The single trap that every small business needs to be aware of is the problem of becoming dependent on a few large customers for a majority of work.

Be concerned if any one customer becomes more than 15 percent of your sales. Red lights should go off when a customer reaches 10 percent of sales, signaling that you should spend more of your time trying to diversify you customer base.

Many small businessmen have been forced into bankruptcy when a single large customer accounted for too much of the company's revenue. A monster customer that has all the cards can and will try to increase its profits at your expense. First the customer will use heavy-handed negotiations to push down its vendor's margins — "take it or we will get someone else." It will then resist any attempt by its smaller dependent vendors to increase prices.

Over time, inflation depletes the small business owner's previously hard-earned capital, until one day... Sound familiar?

THE CUSTOMER ISN'T ALWAYS RIGHT?

No, said Rudy Smith of Rudy Smith Service, Inc., in New Orleans, La. "'The Customer Is Always Right' is bull $#!& !!!"

"There was never a more harmful, misleading idea introduced to the business world," said Smith. "Many in the towing industry accept this as a foregone conclusion and think that there are no other customers to be had."

According to Smith, towing company owners should review their customer lists on a regular basis, evaluate the profitability of each, and identify any that are not contributing to achieving the company's goals.

"The bad customers are usually hiding behind high sales volume with low or no profit margins — or are the type of customer that burn up way too much time with problems and unrealistic expectations," said Smith.

After you've identified your problem accounts, continued Smith, try to rehabilitate those relationships by raising your price and profit margins to compensate for your time and effort. Alternatively you can adjust the customers' expectations to match what they're paying you.

"There will always be customers that won't change," said Smith. "If you find that to be the case, don't waste more time. Fire that customer and use your newly found time to solicit better clients and other opportunities."

Repossession:
A Tough Job for the Right Tower

It's a close cousin to the towing work you already do every day. But it has its own set of rules and its own dangers to those who are involved in it. It's not for everyone — but, done well, it can be an exciting and rewarding line of work for towers who want to expand their client base in a new direction.

Welcome to the world of repossession.

To get a feel for this unique business, we asked for help from several experts. They had a lot of good advice for towers who want to get into repossession work. An important rule of thumb is this:

Repossession is *not* the same thing as towing!

First and foremost, towing company owners must realize that the repossession business is a different animal than what they're used to.

"They really need to do their homework," said Susan Marston, editor-in-chief of TheAmericanRepossessor.com magazine in Ohio, and a former Vice President of a statewide Repossession Company. "They really need to understand what the repossession industry is about, because it's not like the towing industry."

The repossession business, explained Marston, has a completely different client base, marketing, software, training, and requires its own specific skill set.

Ideally, said Marston, a repossession company should be a separate business because when you're marketing your services to financial institutions it's important to establish a clear identity — one that defines your repossession business as a separate entity from your towing business.

The long haul

As with a towing business, building a repossession company can take a while. "It's hard to get clients at the beginning," said Terrance Hill, president of Hill Enterprises, based in Chillicothe, Ohio. "But it pays off in the long run."

Unlike some towers who add repossession work to their list of existing towing services, Hill actually started his career in the repossession field. "When the economy went downhill [recently], I was looking for a job," recalled Hill. "I thought, 'Why not start a towing repo company?'"

Like many newcomers to the business, Hill started his company with one employee — himself — and a single pickup truck. He outfitted his truck with a Minute Man HDH slide-in wheel lift, which gave his fledgling business a lifting capacity of 3,500 pounds and a towing capacity of 7,500 pounds.

Once he got going, "it just went from there," said Hill. Today his company has three trucks: a 2004 Ford F350 quad cab long-bed (with a Minuteman HDH wheel lift installed) and two International rollbacks.

Hill recommends that new repossessors start with a "buy-here-pay-here" car lot that takes care of its own financing. "Get a couple clients that way," said Hill," and start building up so that you have a reputation for yourself. Then you can get other clients."

Also, said Hill, be prepared for long, long hours. "You think towing involves long hours?" he said. "Towing doesn't even compare to repossession. You work extremely long hours, sitting on houses, staking them out, waiting for cars to come."

Do your homework before forging ahead

To assist people who are interested in launching a repossession company, Marston's Web site features an entry titled "So You Want to Start a Repossession Company"— a comprehensive set of 46 questions designed to ensure that the candidate has thought everything through. The list includes the following items to mull over:

- Do you know what form of legal ownership is best for your business?
- Do you know what special licensing or permits are required?
- Do you know what technology you will need to operate and manage your business?
- Do you know where to obtain information about regulations and compliance requirement that impact your business?
- How will you market your company?
- How will you identify the correct repossession insurance and other pertinent insurances?
- Do you have any repossession experience?
- Do you understand the repossession industry?
- What services will the repossession company provide?
- Why are you starting a repossession business?
- Do you understand marketing within the repossession industry?
- Who is your competition?
- What are the unique elements of your business?

Again, it's critical that the business owner understand that running a repossession business is *not* the same as running a towing business. "I would hate to see people lose their money because they say to themselves, 'Well, I've got a tow truck so I should be able to do repossessions,'" said Marston.

High tech repossession

The repossession industry has its own computer software packages that are often used by lenders as well as repossession personnel. According to Marston, some software packages allow clients to view their accounts, allowing the clients to track vehicles that are pending and access other important information. "At the same time," continued Marston, "field agents can see their section, and the administrator can see all sections."

If a repossession company has more than one storage lot, the software can show where each vehicle is stored and for how long. "It's no longer like the old days," said Marston, "when literally it was a case of one man and his truck, and maybe getting a new account via fax."

Many of these software packages are able to receive new account information via the Internet. "Or you can manually enter them in," said Marston. "From there you can assign field agents, send updates, monitor the performance of your account executives, check the account, and see who's doing what on all of your accounts."

Watch the law

Much of the repossession business is a matter of possession: have you taken control of the vehicle in question, or does the owner still have possession? "As long as you throw a chain around one of the tires, that car is in your possession now," explained Hill.

You can contact your local law enforcement agency for guidance on keeping your repossession work honest, and to ensure that you and your employees abide by the law. Some key points, according to Hill: "Don't get caught on the property. Have the collateral in your possession. If they want you off their property, then you have to leave." And to be able to collect the vehicle smoothly and quickly, "the element of surprise is really important," said Hill.

"We provide our services not only for motor vehicles, but anything with wheels," said Hill. "In the repossession world there are many laws and ordinances that must be followed to insure a successful repossession. We record every repo with video and audio which is available upon request to insure a law-abiding repossession."

Don't forget that repossession companies need their own repossession insurance, said Marston. "Repossession insurance is not the same as just having tow insurance," she explained. "Often repossessors have specialized insurance — and it's not cheap!"

Hill mentioned that his company carries $1 million in on-hook insurance and is licensed through the Public Utilities Commission of Ohio and the Ohio Department of Transportation. "Without the proper insurance," said Hill, "your asset could be damaged and not covered."

Watch out for the vehicle owner

If you're taking a vehicle and its owner suddenly appears on scene, things can sometimes get nasty. In these cases it's best to level with the owner. "We just try to keep the situation calm," said Hill. "We tell the person, 'Look, we understand. We're sorry. It's got to be done, though. And you *can* get it back.'"

If being straightforward doesn't calm an irate vehicle owner, Hill typically continues explaining the situation to him or her: "The more we have to do here, the higher the bill is going to be."

Hill sometimes asks the vehicle owner for the keys. "If you give us the keys to your car, we'll let you get your stuff out before we tow it," said Hill. "If not, then we have to inventory everything, and you'll have to pay to get your stuff out of the vehicle."

Outfitting your truck...and more

If you're planning to open your own repossession company, what kind of truck should you use? "What I've found in the repossession industry is that most repossessors have their own favorite make and model of tow trucks and stick to the mix of equipment that they like," said Marston. Most companies, she added, perform repossessions using tow trucks, but some also like to use rollbacks.

What makes a tow truck a "repossession tow truck"? Certain types of towing equipment can help the repossessor do the job quickly — a necessity in a business where timing can be everything when having to take a vehicle away from delinquent but reluctant owner.

At Detroit Wrecker Sales in Michigan, Chris Vanderwalker talks to customers about the type of repossession truck they need. Then he puts together a YouTube "video proposal" to show the customer what trucks and equipment are available for their specific repossession work. "We use YouTube to convey our thoughts," explained Vanderwalker.

The company's YouTube video collection (www.youtube.com/detroitwrecker) also offers on-the-job advice for towers and repossessors. This video communication between Detroit Wrecker and its customers allows the company to disseminate information to the maximum number of people in an economical manner.

With YouTube, said Vanderwalker, "Out-of-state customers take advantage of watching their units being built or installed while sitting in the comfort of their home." Customers can ship their trucks to Detroit Wrecker, where Vanderwalker records the modification process on video and posts it to YouTube. When the work is complete, the truck is shipped back to the customer.

In addition to stocking parts from Jerr-Dan, Miller, Chevron and Dynamic, Detroit Wrecker also manufactures towing equipment. Equipment includes wheel lifts, sling units and flatbeds. According to the company, its Low Loader Flat Bed features the lowest load angle of any flatbed wrecker built in the U.S. This component costs $24,500 installed, and Vanderwalker recommends this product for people getting into the repossession business.

Detroit Wrecker's YouTube channel includes short videos that demonstrate a variety of other wheel lifts recommended for repossessors. These wheel lifts have names such as Lil' Hercules, 601 Slide-In, 601 Stealthand The Holmes 220 Snatcher.

For towers looking to get into the repossession business, Vanderwalker noted that it's a great career for people who are very independent. "It takes hard work, like everything else in life," he said. "You are your own boss and are completely in control of your destiny."

"To start up your career," said Vanderwalker, "you can purchase a sling unit for as little as $3,250 or a wheel lift starting at $4,995."

Don't believe everything you see

If you've watched any of the television series that showcase a repossession outfit, know that the real-life version is leagues removed from its TV portrayal. The repossessions shown on these TV shows are often reenacted after-the-fact, and the drama is amped up for entertainment purposes.

Unfortunately, said Marston, these over-the-top performances by repossession personnel cast a bad light on the industry as a whole. "There's already so much negativity within the industry because of these TV programs," lamented Marston. "I've heard many horror stories where debtors have seen repossessions on TV and expect to be treated the same way if their vehicle is out for repossession."

"These shows are made for TV," continued Marston. "A lot of it is hype. But it is what it is: people watch TV to be entertained."

Viewers who are surprised at the behavior exhibited by repossession personnel on these shows need to remember that they're watching a TV program, said Marston. "From my experience in the industry, 99.9 percent is *nothing* like what you see on TV. If those kinds of things actually happened in real life, clients would close down their contracts with the repossession company in a heartbeat. They would stop giving them work."

"There are so many repossession companies out there that are really professional and provide quality services," said Marston. "They go to great lengths to train their people. They invest in technology. They're very proud of what they do."

Finally, another good piece of advice from a repossession expert: Because you may be waiting long hours in your truck, "get a coffee thermos," said Hill. "That's the best thing I can tell someone who wants to get into the industry."

Another opinion

For a different opinion on this topic, we talked to Dennis Wencel, a tower, author of *The Black Book of Towing*.

Wencel cautions towing company owners who want to move into the repossession business: "Though initially repossession may seem like a natural growth opportunity for a towing company, often it turns out not to be the case," he said. "A few years ago repo work was booming. So many people were defaulting on their loans [that] banks and other lending institutions were scouring the phone books for any towing company willing to reclaim their collateral assets."

For starters, the repossessor's client base is different that what he or she is used to as a tower. In addition to making yourself known to these lenders, explained Wencel, new repossessors also have to adapt to their processes of work assignment, payment routines and paperwork processing.

What's the most frustrating situation in the repossession business? According to Wencel, you may put a lot of work into locating a vehicle — and not end up repossessing it after all. "Either you cannot safely or legally access the vehicle," said Wencel, "or the owner brings their loan current or maybe the car is just never located."

"This is a new reality for towers who like to have a predictable cash flow for work performed," Wencel continued, "even if it is at a less than desirable rate."

In addition, said Wencel, there's a learning curve for the tow truck operator, who now has to tow a vehicle that's in the possession of someone who doesn't *want* it towed.

This means that the tower must learn "to adapt covert strategies for locating the vehicle and know how to identify the most opportune time to attempt the repossession," said Wencel.

"Further, the operator has to be familiar with laws concerning vehicle repossession including breaching the peace and entering private property."

"Then the operator must possess the skills to safely tow a vehicle without keys," continued Wencel. "This will require using go jacks or other car skate products which take time to use and when used in a rush can result in damaged vehicles."

Finally, said Wencel, repossession tows are often performed during late hours when there is less chance of conflict with a vehicle owner. So the typical towing company that performs 90 percent of its work from 7 a.m. to 7 p.m. "must now staff up the overnight crew with operators who possess the above skills, don't mind working in a hostile environment and enjoy working the midnight shift," said Wencel.

"Certainly some towers have found success in this area but it requires the tower to adapt to a whole new skill set," said Wencel.

Motor Clubs: Towing Partners

Imagine working with motor clubs for nearly four decades. It's an impressive statistic for any tower. Anthony Gentile, owner of Dynamic Towing Equipment in Norfolk, Va., has had contracts with clubs such as Allstate, Geico, Cross Country, and Nationwide. Gentile maintained these motor club contracts out of his towing company in New York City.

How did Gentile get started in the motor club business? At the beginning of his career, "the station where I worked [in New York] was a AAA station," recalled Gentile. When Gentile later purchased that station, he continued the motor club contract that was already in place.

What's it like to work for a motor club? We talked to several of the top clubs in the country to see how they select their towing service providers — and how the motor clubs do business in a very competitive environment.

FleetNet

More than 3,000 towing companies comprise FleetNet's network in the U.S. and Canada. However, the Cherryville, N.C.-based company isn't strictly a motor club.

"We are the largest medium- and heavy-duty nationwide towing network, among other things," explained Heather Holt, the company's director of marketing.

Holt said that FleetNet America is a third-party maintenance management company that coordinates emergency roadside service and maintenance management services for all types of vehicles except automobiles. Holt added that FleetNet's vendors do not pay a fee to join the network.

FleetNet's services are available 24 hours a day, seven days a week, throughout the United States and Canada. "We are responsible for nearly 300,000 events annually and manage over 500,000 vehicles," said Holt.

Of the 300,000 events each year, said Holt, more than 34,500 are towing-related. Those events involve any of the following: tows, winch-outs, accidents, swap-outs, load shifts, pull starts, and jumpstarts.

Road America

At Road America, based in Miami, Fla., contracted towers primarily handle jobs such as emergency response services, accidents, secondary towing and salvage transport.

"Our network coverage varies greatly according to client/fleet geographical distribution," said Marci Kleinsasser, director of marketing and client services for Road America. "We cover the U.S., Canada, and Puerto Rico through our North America regional office, and worldwide through our Mafpre Asistencia affiliated offices." (The Mapfre Group, the largest insurance company in Spain, is the parent company of Road America.)

Call volume at Road America varies according to geographical area and season, said Kleinsasser. The club's highest call volume occurs during the summer months.

Agero (formerly Cross Country)

After nearly four decades, the Cross Country motor club recently changed its name to Agero (from the Latin word *agere*, meaning "to do, to lead, to drive"). Gary Wallace, vice president of corporate relations for the company, praised the company's network of towers: "Agero has been fortunate with the volume of participants throughout the country in its network of service providers from the towing and the roadside industry."

While corporate policy precludes Agero from specifying how many towing companies it contracts with, the company says its network is "quite robust" and provides assistance to more than 75 million customers annually.

"We hold our service providers to a very high standard of customer service and service delivery when they work with us," noted Wallace.

"We have high expectations for the service and experience that is delivered," continued Wallace. "In turn, we want to make attaining the resources and information necessary for our providers to execute on this delivery as easy for them to access as possible."

The American Automobile Association

Sandi Rauch, marketing and communications manager for the AAA National Office in Santa Ana, Calif., noted that AAA's organization is decentralized: it's a network of independently-owned and operated motor clubs, each handling its own specific geographical area.

According to Rauch, each affiliated AAA club is the sole decision-maker regarding the cost of membership and the receiving and dispatching of calls for roadside assistance. In addition, the individual clubs handle all of their own contractual and business decisions with road service providers, including qualifications and rates.

"The combined road service network of all AAA clubs includes some 8,000 independent contractors," said Rauch. "AAA's service network and membership are nationwide in both the U.S. and Canada. The association recently surpassed 53 million members in the North America."

When it comes to selecting towing vendors, each AAA club makes its decisions based on geographic and other needs, explained Rauch.

"Compensation plans are set by the clubs and will vary; many AAA clubs provide service providers the opportunity to earn additional incentives. Actual details vary by AAA club."

Getting into the club

Gentile pointed to the steady paycheck and consistent amount of work as two big reasons why working with motor clubs is a plus for towing companies.

In selecting new service providers, companies such as FleetNet start with an interview. FleetNet also contacts members of its current customer base that are located in the same geographic areas as the prospective vendor, explained Holt. This allows FleetNet to obtain further reference information. The company also talks to state towing associations and the Towing & Recovery Association of America (TRAA) to locate good qualified vendors.

"We attend several trade shows per year and receive referrals from customers and other vendors to add new vendors to our network," continued Holt. "We also verify the vendor's Department of Transportation number on the Federal Motor Carrier Safety Administration Web site."

Once a towing company becomes a FleetNet vendor, the tower is rated based on factors such as performance, quality of work, availability, insurance, and rates.

Agero's basic philosophy for selecting towers is similar. "Our number-one emphasis when recruiting new service providers is ensuring that they have the ability to provide customers with the best roadside experience possible, every time," explained Wallace. "Proper training and high customer service standards are key to joining our network and stressed for every provider with whom we work."

Struggling with setting rates

For towers who have issues with one or more motor clubs but don't feel like they're being heard, a new organization is offering its assistance. Last January almost 75 towing companies gathered in Sacramento, Calif., at a meeting for the United Coalition for Motor Club Safety. UCMCS will serve as a single voice for towers' concerns.

The clubs are, of course, aware that not every vendor is a happy one. Agero, for example, hosts periodic discussions with the participants in its network regarding the rates and volume of tows and roadside events that are made available, said Wallace. "Our goal is to make working with Agero as beneficial to our service providers as possible, saving them time and money along the way."

"During negotiations," said Kleinsasser of Road America, "we agree to rates that are both, fair and competitive, because we know that in order to receive the highest service quality, providers must be compensated fairly for their hard work."

According to Holt, FleetNet negotiates rates with individual vendors to stay competitive in each region. Since it's not a motor club in the traditional sense, Holt noted that the company uses independent vendors as well as original equipment manufacturer (OEM) dealers — truck, trailer and refrigeration.

"We do not set rates for the vendors to charge," explained Holt. "We want a partnership with our vendors and want them to make money. Also — which is very important — we pay vendors in a timely manner for their work. A vendor is able to choose various payment terms based on their contract."

Regarding towers' complaints about rates set by some of the motor clubs, Kleinsasser noted that the clubs are in a quandary too. "The truth of the matter is providers will always feel 'squeezed,'" she said, "and it is understandable considering the decrease in profit margins associated with ever-increasing costs.Road America values greatly its relationship with all service partners and is committed to paying the highest feasible rates."

"We appreciate that like all companies, service providers are focused on the profitability of their business," said Wallace of Agero/Cross Country."We are committed to providing tools and other resources to our network participants to improve their operational efficiencies and increase their bottom line profits."

Getting involved

For towers interested in becoming a service provider, Gentile offered this advice: "Call them. See them at tow shows. Network yourself a little bit. Learn their requirements."

Also, note that a vendor's contract with a motor club can involve a lot more than just towing. Gentile pointed to service trucks as a growing part of the motor clubs' offerings to their clients. Among other assistance, the service trucks provide roadside battery installation for dead vehicles.

Gentile's company, Dynamic Towing Equipment, builds tow trucks. In addition, Dynamic produces "a [service] truck with a racking system to hold the batteries in place," explained Gentile, "plus a wheel lift on the back." That way, he said, if the operator installs a new battery but the vehicle still won't run, then the vehicle can simply be towed away.

Working with a motor club is "another way to get work into the shop," noted Gentile. It's not for everybody, he added, but it's worked out well for his business for nearly forty years.

Towing Associations: Bringing Everyone (and Everything) Together

Whether you join up to take classes, share ideas, meet other towers, or participate in the annual tow show, every towing association offers a variety of programs and activities to improve your business. What you may not know is just how challenging the logistics of running an association can be.

We talked to a number of towing associations across the country to get a snapshot of what it's like to support thousands of members in the industry. We also took a look at some of the unique programs that towing associations across the nation are sponsoring for their members, families and communities.

Running a tow show

The logistics involved in creating and executing a tow show — whether it's a state or regional event — are enormous. "The number one challenge is the *time* it takes to do a good show," said Mike Walcker, director of the Towing and Recovery Association of Washington. Solid leadership can save the day. TRAW, for example, has two co-chairs — Dan Johnson and Jackie Currie — for its Northwest Tow Expo. Johnson and Currie have organized the show for the past three years. (They also serve on TRAW's staff as president and treasurer, respectively.

The next challenge to running a good tow show, said Walcker, is finding and keeping a good venue. TRAW hosts its show at the Silver Reef Casino, a 50,000 square foot facility in Ferndale, Wash., that features a 150-room hotel, seven restaurants, an events facility and a spa. "We are fortunate that we have found and kept a good quality, well-balanced and affordable site that caters to our show year after year," said Walcker.

Jess Horton, president of the Southwest Tow Operators, listed five key issues that tow show planners face:

1. *Money*, which must be fronted for extended periods of time to get the show up and running. "Where does it come from, and who is keeping track?" said Horton.

2. *Volunteers* who can give up time they would have spent enjoying the show and instead work at the show.

3. *Selling the show to potential vendors.* "You literally have to travel to *other* shows and recruit [in order to] gain enough vendors to support the show," explained Horton. "Then, after you sell the booth, you have to ask for sponsorship dollars as well."

4. *Liaising with government.* You need to deal with city or county employees (or other government officials) to obtain the required permits. State officials, for example, may want permits for trucks, special equipment, training areas, and other items.

5. *Enough bang for the buck.* It's critical, said Horton, to make sure that "the attendees will get the most out of the experience, without breaking their banks at the same time."

The financial investment in a tow show can be tricky because it comes "without a guarantee of return," noted Tom Brennan, president of the Empire State Towing and Recovery Association. In addition, Mother Nature can crumple your best efforts: "The success and attendance of the show can be dependent on the weather," said Brennan.

Sometimes even a successful show can trigger new problems for the host organization. For example, the Northwest Tow Expo has gradually outgrown its traditional location. "We are approaching maximum capacity for our venue site," explained Walcker. "Last year we had 205 seated dinner guests at the banquet in a room with a maximum capacity of 200." The Silver Reef Casino is constructing additional facilities, added Walcker, "but we seem to be keeping up with all they can give us."

Celebrity auctions and racecar experiences

Another challenge in hosting a tow show: keeping it interesting for the attendees. Rene Fortin, president of the New Hampshire Towing Association, points to his organization's upcoming event, the 40th Annual Family Tow & and Trade Show, which will feature the Richard Petty Driving Experience. For $79 attendees can drive or ride along in a NASCAR racecar on the New Hampshire Motor Speedway.

In 2010, the Towing and Recovery Association of Ohio kicked off a new tradition at its annual Midwest Regional Tow Show: the Celebrity Auction. "We always change things up so it doesn't get boring," said Donna Brock-Mesaros, administrator for the Association.

"We were looking for a fundraiser to fund our Ohio Injured Driver's Fund," explained Mesaros. While researching possible options, Mesaros stumbled across the idea for a celebrity auction. She had to find a sponsor and an auctioneer. Mesaros turned to her husband Don — coincidentally, the president of TRAO — and nudged him a bit. "I explained to my husband that I needed an auctioneer," said Mesaros, "and that he would be great!"

However, her husband's initial response wasn't quite what she was looking for. "The look he gave me was priceless!" laughed Mesaros. "I was looking for someone with personality who would know the bidders and could call them by name." After some discussion, Don agreed to take the job.

In 2011 AAA Allied Group came on board as the sponsor of the auction. Notable items included:

- Framed tow truck license plates and a bronze tow truck, donated by Miller Industries

- $2,000 donated by Jerr-Dan
- Cap autographed by comedian Larry the Cable Guy
- Harmonica autographed by country artist Clint Black
- Framed comic books of the movie "Cars," autographed by Larry the Cable Guy
- A weekend package at the Great Wolf Lodge Indoor Water Park Resort, valued at $1,500
- Dallas Cowboys 50th Anniversary football autographed by quarterback Tony Romo
- Poster for the animated movie "Cars 2," autographed by voice actors Larry the Cable Guy, John Lasseter, Emily Mortimer, Owen Wilson and Michael Caine. (This item was purchased by George & Cindy Connolly and Don & Donna Mesaros, who donated it to the International Towing and Recovery Hall of Fame and Museum in Chattanooga, Tenn.)
- Eyeglasses donated by actor Martin Sheen, worn in the TV series "The West Wing"
- Footballs autographed by Cincinnati Bengal cornerback Leon Hall and Cleveland Browns wide receiver Joshua Cribbs
- Book, CD and photo donated by media personality Glenn Beck
- Book autographed by actor Henry Winkler ("Happy Days," "Arrested Development")
- Topps sports card donated by golfer Tiger Woods

The results of the event were impressive. During the initial auction in 2010 TRAO raised $5,000. By the next year the auction generated three times that amount. Because the sponsor of the action covers framing, food and beverage costs, "100 percent of the money raised goes to our Injured Drivers Fund," explained Mesaros, "and is distributed to Ohio towers (non-members included) who are killed in the line of duty and to members who are injured and out of work for at least two weeks."

"In September of last year — about three weeks prior to TRAO's annual tow show — Ohio lost a driver who was killed while sweeping up after an accident," said Mesaros. "This was a non-member who received a check from the Ohio Injured Driver's Fund for $1,000." Mesaros added that the fund is not intended to replace workers' compensation payments but to aid the employee and family while he or she is awaiting the check.

Volunteers

Nonprofit organizations — towing associations included — often require a small army of volunteers to assist with everything from running the office to overseeing the tow shows. Brennan noted that Empire State Association members "travel at their own expense to meetings, seminars, training and other tow shows.Our tow show depends on volunteers for setup, staffing and organizing events for the show."

Although the Southwest Tow Operators is fortunate to have a full-time paid staff, Horton noted that volunteers drive the organization. "We hold many meetings all over the state of Texas, and it is the volunteer that brings everything together and cleans up afterwards." Horton added that the volunteers bring legislators, sheriffs, police chiefs, mayors, judges, and other towing industry people to meetings and other association events.

At the Towing and Recovery Association of Ohio, the board, membership and volunteers make the organization. An average of 75 volunteers help with the annual Midwest Regional Tow Show and with community service activities. The 2011 "Towers Support Our Troops" program collected 10 moving boxes of items to ship to American troops deployed overseas. TRAO's volunteers also gathered and transported toys for children of families devastated by the tornado in Joplin, Mo., in 2011.

Scholarships and the school board

The Towing and Recovery Association of Kentucky sponsors scholarship programs for local students. Headed by Nick Schade, TRAK boasts more than 650 towing operators among its members. Recently TRAK's treasurer, Scott Burrows, came up with a fresh approach to the organization's scholarship program that brought two important state associations — one representing the towing industry, the other a school board — together.

A number of years ago, TRAK awarded scholarships to deserving high school seniors, with funds generated from the interest on corporate funds. "I had served on several of the scholarship committees in the past and was acquainted with the process," recalled Burrows.

However, Burrows continued, the scholarships were somewhat

difficult to manage and award. Each of the scholarship applications had to be vetted, and then the committee chose a winner or winners from the approved applicants. "This was cumbersome to those association members who already had their plates full with other responsibilities," explained Burrows.

In addition, said Burrows, tow truck drivers may have not been the best choice for determining the award recipients, as most (if not all) of them had little background in classifying, deconstructing and evaluating scholarship applications.

Burrows had served on his local school board for more than six years and was also on the board of the directors for the Kentucky School Boards Association (KSBA). Burrows felt that if TRAK and the School Boards Association joined forces, the resulting scholarship program would benefit greatly.

TRAK already had a funding mechanism in place: a percentage of membership dues were designated for continuing education for members and their dependents. "We commit funds to solicit training for our members," explained Burrows, "and we return the members investments in TRAK (their dues payments) to them in this manner, as well as in the distribution of scholarship funds to their family members."

Burrows' idea took hold. KSBA presented the two most recent scholarship recipients — high school seniors Kelsey Rae Bentley and Dustin Tyler Adams — $2,500 scholarships last February during the annual KSBA conference in Louisville, Ky. Burrows noted that nearly 600 school board members and administrators attended the conference. "I think it was a good opportunity to get the positive exposure for our towing association to the educational community," said Burrows.

For the future, Burrows is looking at ways to expand the scholarship program. He contacted the Kentucky Motor Transport Association, whose executive director Jamie Fiepke was interested in hearing more. "They have some under-utilized funding for scholarships available," said Burrows, who added that if TRAK and KMTA can combine efforts, it "could make a greater impact on the scholarship program."

Programs for fun and education

Associations are also heavily involved in providing training and education for their members. In addition to its monthly district meetings held from September through May of each year, the Towing and Recovery Association of Washington sponsors four light-duty schools, one medium-duty school and one heavy-duty school, plus an additional three or four one-day schools, said Walcker.

In May TRAW hosts a spring education meeting, gathering six to eight professional instructors from a variety of areas (state labor and industries, ecology, state patrol) and private business (tire experts, fuel experts, certified mailing company). "[They] give an all-day educational opportunity for our guests at no cost," explained Walcker, "then have a nice banquet with a guest speaker and entertainment."

Members can also look forward to association events that provide for rest and relaxation. Walcker said that TRAW hosts an annual Winter Festival each January that offers a getaway in the resort town of Lake Chelan, "where we have first class accommodations for a fraction of the normal rate, a very nice banquet and tons of fun and relaxation."

Regional or state shows?

"I think of tow shows as a window into the future of our industry," said Horton. Does that future include shows on the regional or state level? Or will both types continue to coexist?

According to Brennan, head of the Empire State Towing and Recovery Association, "State shows are the way to go. "The state show, continued Brennan, "benefits your local association. In our case, the funds realized help run the association for the year and target education for state and local laws."

By contrast, Mesaros felt that regional events were more beneficial. "Manufacturers and exhibitors want regional shows," said Mesaros. "To secure the exhibitors you need towers attending, and to secure the attendance you need the exhibitors."

Horton agreed, noting that regional shows are the best platforms for towers and vendors. "It brings more towers together and allows for a better atmosphere for all involved," he explained. However, Horton added that Southwest Tow Operators also hosts smaller local events for its members —small picnics held throughout the state of Texas. "One of the largest we have is called the Southwest Pachanga, held down in South Texas (Region 4) every year." Several hundred attendees and their families typically attend this event.

Because no tow shows occur in Oregon or Idaho, the Towing and Recovery Association of Washington feels that its annual get-together is "truly a regional show," said Walcker. The 2011 show hosted guests from China, Canada and Australia, as well as attendees from the United States. "We considered our show more of an international show than even a regional show," added Walcker. "Our proximity to Canada is a great benefit as we always have a good showing from our friends from the North."

Southwest Tow Operators takes a completely different approach to its tow show: it doesn't directly host it. "We've taken the stance from the very beginning of our organization that associations should not be operating tow shows," said Horton. "STO has always believed that the association's attentions and energy should be focused on the members and the needs of those members."

Although STO doesn't independently host tow shows, Horton stressed that the association is nevertheless a huge proponent of these events. "We do believe in the tow show," he said, "just not in us running it." To that end, STO partnered with *American Towman* magazine, "an existing company that coordinates successful tow shows already," said Horton, including the Baltimore Tow Show. This partnership, Horton said, has allowed STO to hold training classes, seminars, certification, meetings and special events "with ease and very little cost" to the association.

Top reasons to join a towing association

Donna Mesaros, administrator for the Towing and Recovery Association of Ohio:

1. Free driver training (two classes each year)

2. The Ohio Injured Driver's Fund, which financially supports operators and their families in case of death or injury

3. Strength in numbers

4. Monthly newsletters

5. Quality leadership

Jess Horton, president of Southwest Tow Operators:

1. Communication. The towing industry lacks adequate communication. This needs to change, and the associations are the ones to make this happen — not just in communication with each other, but also with other stakeholders involved and around our industry.

2. Creating unity, strength, common purpose and goals ("one voice"). By coming together, we've proven over and over that this industry *can* get things done. The problem is that most of the time things fall apart again until the "next big thing" comes along. We need long-lasting and consistent unity that brings forth constant, positive things to the industry.

3. Legislative and regulatory issues. Consistent monitoring and lobbying is needed, not only to fight bad elements when they come at our industry but also to promote positive elements consistently and to educate those who make the laws and rules that regulate us. We need to challenge questionable issues *before* they become *big* issues.

4. Training and knowledge building. Not just "how-to" about tow trucks, but also for business applications, safety, etc. We need to invite people in the industry to promote existing knowledge, and also promote persons from outside of the industry to gain that fresh perspective — that "out of the box" approach.

Top 5 challenges to running a tow show

Donna Mesaros, administrator for the Towing and Recovery Association of Ohio:

1. Organizing each event individually

2. Organizing the volunteers

3. Overall planning of the event

4. Adding something new each year to the schedule
5. Ideal location

Tom Brennan, president of the Empire State Towing and Recovery Association:
1. Vendor solicitation
2. Affordability to the attendees
3. Securing enough volunteers to staff the event
4. Selecting a venue that provides a vacation atmosphere for families to attract more attendees
5. Providing unique educational activities

Top 5 reasons tow shows are important

Tom Brennan, president of the Empire State Towing and Recovery Association, picked his top five highlights of the tow show experience. Tow shows...
1. Exhibit state-of-the-art products.
2. Provide opportunity for towers to exchange ideas and talk about the industry.
3. Provide a venue for training.
4. Provide vendors an opportunity to reach customers.
5. Provide towers an opportunity to see new products and get discounts from vendors.

Signage: Keeping it Effective and Legal

Every interaction with a customer (or potential customer) makes an impression of some type. If you answer a customer's questions clearly and honestly, that's a point in your favor. If your vehicles and staff appear sharp, clean and professional, you'll be remembered. When you complete a recovery job efficiently and safely, customers will spread the word.

Then there's the visual aspect of your business — the signage that conveys the nature of your work. Are the signs and graphics on your shop and vehicles colorful? Easy to see from a distance? Memorable for their artwork or logos? So snazzy that customers can't help but remember them?

Those signs on your buildings and trucks should never be taken for granted. The best mix of qualities for effective signage: attractive, eye-catching design that complies with local and state regulations. In some cases, balancing these two requirements can be quite a challenge for towing companies.

171

Designing signs that pop

Sign*A*Rama in Leesburg, Va., touts itself as the largest full-service sign center in the world. The company has created paint schemes for a number of local towing companies. "As with all design," said John Voigt, president of Sign*A*Rama, "a good sign comes from understanding the message it needs to present and the audience its intended for."

According to Voigt, clarity is achieved by using clean, easy to read fonts and by using color combinations that give good contrast. "Incorporating logos to increase branding and adding playful or unusual elements gives a sign that is memorable," added Voigt.

Minimizing clutter is also important, according to Leslie Goolsby, president of Anchor Graphics, Inc., in McKinney, Texas. Goolsby's company creates signs and graphics for towing companies across the country. "We have found that less is more," said Goolsby. "The less you put on the sign, the more likely they are to read it."

Customers may indeed turn away from your shop if they can't find the name of the business over the door, or if the signage looks amateurish or tattered. Towers may work on asphalt, in dirt and grime, and in all sorts of harsh weather conditions — but it's still critical to keep outward appearances as clean and welcoming as possible. In a down economy, with customers keeping a tight hold on their wallets, keeping your signage looking good could even mean the difference between staying open or closing down.

Private property signage

Many states and local governments have specific guidelines with regard to signage, said Michael McGovern, an attorney and former tower in Knoxville, Tenn., who recently published his new book *Towing and the Law: A Collection of 101 Informative Articles*. According to McGovern, regulated items include the size of the sign, reflection, size of lettering, precise language on sign, and the placement and number of signs.

"Even in those states or cities that do not specifically require signage prior to removal of trespassing, I recommend the use of them," said

McGovern. "It can avoid a lot of later confrontation if the vehicle driver ignored a plainly posted 'no parking' sign."

In Sligo, Ky., owner Scott Burrows and his family have dealt with signage issues since their shop opened in 1917. "It is imperative that signs be posted according to the legal requirements of the jurisdiction that has authority over the parking areas being posted," said Burrows.

Burrows offered the following tips for private property signs: "[They] need to be plainly legible — and that (almost always) mandates plain block lettering, of a size readily readable from the parking area. This may be stated in the regulations that apply to permit parking." Also, said Burrows, consider the language requirements of the people who will read the signs you're posting. In areas where people don't speak much English, bilingual signs are extremely useful.

Jeanette Rash, owner of Fast Tow in Houston, Texas, has dealt with private property towing — and all of the ups and downs therein — during her many years in the business. The state of Texas mandates a standardized design scheme for signage dealing with private property towing. Rash referred to Chapter 2308 of the state Occupations Code, which deals with vehicle towing and booting.

The point of the law, said Rash, "was to have uniform signs for private properties statewide so that when a person saw that 'red-and-white sign with the tow symbol,' you would know that towing on that property is possible."

"We passed the uniform signs here in Texas years ago and they are specific," continued Rash. "No other signs comply. All sign companies caught on long time ago. The only problem is that occasionally a property owner doesn't want red and white as it doesn't 'match' their decor."

If you hunt for regulations and can't find any, said McGovern, "I would recommend that the tower follow the sign guidelines set forth in those jurisdictions where there *are* specific criteria."

For example, said McGovern, the state of Tennessee has no statewide guidelines. "A tow operator in Tennessee in a town with no local requirements might want to look at the Florida statute for guidance," explained McGovern.

"Also, there are several towing sign companies that could be of help in designing a sign," said McGovern. For example, as part of its service to customers, Anchor Graphics does its best to keep track of each state's signage requirements.

Towers who blow off legal requirements or fail to follow the law carefully could find themselves in court. For private property towing, "proper signage can avoid lawsuits," said McGovern, "and can [help you] avoid being sued under the state consumer protection laws, which often allow for treble (triple) damages plus an award of attorney's fees."

"I have also represented towing companies in California that have been charged *criminally* for violating that state's private property tow-away law, including the signage rules," noted McGovern.

Wrapping graphics around a tow truck

According to Voigt, creating signage for tow trucks can be a challenge due to the lack of flat surfaces on the vehicles. "Incorporating the interesting vehicle shape into the overall graphics design helps leave a lasting impression," explained Voigt. "High contrast (including perhaps reflective graphics) increases readability and safety — particularly at night."

Voigt noted that the two most important elements in a tow truck graphics scheme are the company name and phone number. When towing companies contact Sign*A*Rama to discuss decorating their trucks, Voigt reminds his customers that graphics need to be readable when the vehicles are moving at high rates of speed, so excess visual clutter around the company name and phone number is best avoided.

"Truck graphics are an entirely different animal," said Burrows. "Many tow operators display their personality, their achievements, their aspirations or their inspirations in truck graphics. One needs to look no farther than advertising pages in this or other towing publications to see a painter's palette of colors, styles and themes."

Burrows felt that it's important for the company name and phone number (or Web site) to be prominent and in contrasting colors. "Some motorists may only get a glance," said Burrows, "so the name and a catchy contact number or Web address — *i.e.*, 1-xxx-WE-TOW-YOU or www. hook-line-and-sinker.com — may be remembered much longer than an eye-grabbing graphic."

Finally, added Burrows, "Nothing shows up better in night photographs than the boldly placed name in reflective materials. An otherwise dark photo has the name and/or phone number jump off the page of a photo of a well-marked tow truck!"

Marketing: going to the experts

In an industry where multiple towing companies compete for business in the same city, getting the word out can be tricky. Here, sign companies can also help. "To increase branding," said Voigt, "the first question is usually about any existing trucks the company has in service and whether there is an existing logo." If there is no logo, Voigt continued, his company tries to help the customer decide if he or she wants a logo designed — either by Sign*A*Rama or by some other commercial logo designer — or whether the customer just wants a basic text design.

Text designs are simpler and cheaper because they involve selecting fonts and colors to represent the company. By contrast, logo designs involve the creation of artwork in addition to choosing fonts and colors. For example, an artist might draw or paint one or more elements of the design. While this approach is more labor intensive and expensive, the end result — an original, designed-from-scratch logo — can be a more effective piece of advertising than a sign with just text on it.

"Some customers come in with clear ideas about what they want; others have no idea," said Voigt. "We always try and steer customers to a design that will help them be successful. We also ask for their budget as it can be a major [issue] in how complex a design they can afford."

But again, to hammer home a critical point: "Make sure before you have signs made that you check with your local city, county and state to make sure there are no requirements or that you are in compliance," said Goolsby. Good design and compliance with the law will ensure that your signs are noticed and are an effective tool in your day-to-day business.

Get the Word Out:
Advertising Tricks and Tips for Towers

Whether you've just launched a new towing and recovery business or have been in the industry for a long time, your advertising campaign can mean the difference between keeping the doors open — and shutting down for good.

When planning your outreach efforts, it's helpful to review both classic and cutting-edge methods of getting the word out to potential customers. we checked in with several towers and vendors to see what techniques they're using to boost business in their local communities and nationwide.

Employees: your most important advertising

Your company's image is critical in establishing a solid relationship with your customers, and first impressions are important. Your drivers are responsible for providing that first impression when they respond to calls. Mike Patellis, owner of Alpha Towing, Inc., in Marietta, Ga., recommends that each driver be dressed in a sharp uniform, with his or her name labeled on the shirt.

Dennis Wencel, towman and author of *The Black Book of Towing*, agrees. "Even though towing is a dirty business, driver/operator appearance is important," he said. Wencel uses something he calls "The Mother Test." "Would I be willing to send a driver and truck to tow my Mom?" he explained. "If the answer is no, chances are that something must be improved."

Uniform subscription programs are affordable, continued Wencel, who added that towers should pay close attention to personal hygiene and also wash their trucks daily to maintain a good appearance while on the road. Patellis recommends that each driver carry his or her own company business card.

"A clean truck and a nice handshake are worth more than $1,000 a month in advertising!" said Patellis.

In and around the shop

Signage, on your building and your vehicles, is also critical when you're trying to attract new customers. Patellis recommends that you place an eye-catching company sign on the street or in front of the office — "[something] neat looking and not made with spray paint." To boost his company's roadside presence, Patellis installed bright neon signs in the windows of his facility. "It looks nice, bright, and clean looking," he explained.

Using your shop as a gathering place for current and potential clients can also bring new business through the doors. At B/A Products Co. in Columbia, Md., co-owner Fritz Dahlin sponsors familiarization classes for towers. While presenting towers important information about different types, grades and ratings of chain, web and wire rope, the classes also feature items sold by B/A Products including custom chains, wire rope and web assemblies.

For Dahlin, who teaches the classes with Chip Kauffman, vice president of B/A Products Co., the classes are an effective way of introducing towers to the company's inventory.

178

B/A Products also sponsors an open house every year at the American Towman show in Baltimore, Md. "We have involved some of the local fire departments' rescue squads, who give demonstrations," said Dahlin. "While many of the attendees are from out of the area, we have used local towing companies to give demonstrations and provide interesting equipment to use our displays."

During the open house Dahlin also performs live break testing of the company's products and gives tours of the factory. "The big finale of the open house is the charity auction," he added, "with all proceeds going to the Survivor Fund and the International Towing Museum." Recently the auction raised over $15,000.

Traveling billboards

Remember also that your company vehicles are advertising tools all by themselves. "Your trucks are rolling billboards," said Wencel. "For many towing companies they, along with the driver/operators, are the most visual aspect of the business." Patellis urges owners to put the name of their company on at least three of the four sides of each truck.

To draw the most attention on the road, pick an eye-catching color scheme for your vehicles. "So many tow trucks are black, red or white," said Wencel. "Just giving your trucks a brightly colored paint job can really make them stand out." Wencel recommended that towers take care of this whenever they get a new vehicle. "This is a nominal upgrade when you order your truck from the factory," he said.

Finally, remember that your vehicles don't have to be in motion to generate interest from potential customers. "If you're not using all your fleet," said Patellis, "park your trucks where the public can see them."

Reaching out online

Having a company Web site "is a no-brainer," said Patellis. According to Wencel, an effective Web site should present the towing company in a favorable, professional light and demonstrate both the capabilities and professionalism of the company and its staff.

"Showing images of clean trucks and talking about your involvement in the local community will vastly improve your position as a local trustworthy company," continued Wencel. "This reduces the anxiety people feel in choosing a tower. Often, [customers] will view this company as a premium service provider and be willing to pay more for the 'quality brand.'"

Online directories can prove useful when customers are trying to find a local towing company. One such directory is towing.com, a Web site where customers can locate towing and other roadside services by performing a simple search based on service type and zip code.

Local community involvement

Working with events and organizations in your local community is another way to put your company name in front of everyone. For example, B/A Products Co. sponsors recreational and high school sports teams in its hometown of Columbia, Md. "We buy ads in programs or banners to hang on fences at the fields," explained Dahlin.

B/A Products also supports fundraising efforts for the Wounded Warrior Project, a nonprofit organization that helps injured veterans through a wide variety of programs. "We pay for the fuel for a race car," said Dahlin, who admits that his company doesn't do this so much for the advertising exposure as to give back to the community.

How did Dahlin's company get involved with auto racing? He and his sons are involved in a series called The 24 Hours of LeMons, which takes place at racetracks across the U.S. "It's an endurance race for cars costing $500 or less," explained Dahlin. "The group we race with built the car out of their own pocket, several companies donated parts such as the roll cage and safety gear, and the race organizers waived entry fees."

Veterans of the wars in Iraq and Afghanistan were given the opportunity to drive the car 10 laps for free. Then, "for a $100 donation to the Wounded Warrior Fund, non-veterans got 10 laps (about 30 minutes of track time)," said Dahlin. "We raised just over $6,000 and had an absolute blast!"

Getting that phone call

Very few customers will have your office phone number at their fingertips. However, there's a way to ensure that everyone remembers your digits. 1-800-RESCUE911, a company based in St. Petersburg, Fla., offers towing companies the opportunity to "rent" the 1-800-RESCUE911 number in the geographical areas they service. The 800 number can then be painted or decaled on the company's tow trucks and service vehicles.

"We're completely different from any other 800 number out there," said Dane Marshlack, president of 1-800-RESCUE911. By advertising its own 800 number, explained Marshlack, a towing company will boost its revenue. "They're going to get more phone calls — full-retail, emergency roadside service calls that are non-discounted, non-motor club type calls."

Echoing Wencel's and Patellis' comments about using vehicles as mobile billboards, Marshlack noted that you can view this as a sort of "guerrilla marketing." Every one of those vehicles in your fleet, said Marshlack, is a double-sided billboard.

"With a powerful phone number that's easy to remember, your company vehicles running around town have thousands of eyeballs looking at them every day," said Marshlack. "That's thousands of impressions every 24 hours." ("Impressions" is a buzzword referring to the number of times a potential customer views an advertisement.)

Marshlack notes that the rule of thumb for potential customers is that "if you see something three times, you're more comfortable with buying it."

The 1-800-RESCUE911 number rings directly at the towing company rather than going through a call center or dispatcher. In addition, the towing company can track incoming calls via Internet-based reporting software. If the dispatcher is busy on another line when a new call comes in, the software automatically captures the number so the dispatcher can call back later.

"There are 3,140 counties in the United States," said Marshlack. "Imagine every county having the 800-RESCUE-911 assigned to a particular tower. When a vehicle owner breaks down, whether it's in Los Angeles, Florida or Texas, he or she can call the same toll-free number to

181

get a tow. And towers get instant credibility with an 800 number of their own, even if they only have one or two trucks."

All towing companies, no matter how large or how small, have a variety of creative advertising methods available to them. Some, such as phone book listings and building signage, have been around for decades. Other methods, such as mobile phone advertising, appeared in the last decade or so and are still being developed and updated.

Regardless of what avenues you take, make sure that you follow through on your efforts. Referring to his company's advertising approach, Patellis noted that "it works, but you must also be consistent."

Mike's list of advertising

Mike Patellis, owner of Alpha Towing, Inc., in Marietta, Ga., recommends the following items as part of your advertising approach:

- Join local civic organizations
- Have a company page on Facebook
- Place a stack of your business cards at other businesses in the area
- Distribute stickers, pens, calendars, hats, key chains
- Web site ("a no-brainer," said Patellis)
- Online advertising with Google and Yahoo
- Company listing in local phone books
- And if you can afford them: local radio station or newspaper advertisements

Driving customer demand

When planning where to place your advertising dollars, it's important to understand how your customers decide on which towing company to contact when they need one.

According to Dennis Wencel, author of *The Black Book of Towing*, customers worry about making the wrong choice, which is why image and branding are so important for a towing company. "The customer wants to choose a company they can trust," explained Wencel, "so building a strong brand that stands out can really increase the calls coming in."

Choosing a towing company is an event-based decision, said Wencel.

"As such, the most effective marketing tools are those that position you on or near the resource people use to solve their problem."

Today, the main resource that customers use is the Internet. "With the increase in effectiveness of search providers to deliver accurate and reliable local business information," explained Wencel, "local search has become the most effective way for a tower to drive calls to their business. The tools are highly targetable and often are pay-per-performance based. That is, you only pay when someone clicks on your ad. The most effective tools for this are Google Adwords and Bing/Yahoo Search Marketing."

Smartphone apps

When someone's vehicle conks out and requires a tow, what's the first thing the vehicle owner does? Typically he or she reaches for a cell phone and starts to hunt for a towing company.

Mobile phone applications can help customers find a tow when they need one. An iPhone application, Tow Truck Finder by Exact Magic Software in Austin, Texas, costs 99 cents and locates towing companies by city, state, country, or zip code. RepairPal, available for the Android and iPhone, helps the user find a repair shop, get estimates, and find a tow truck. Other applications, both free and low-cost, are available for different brands of smartphone.

Defining your service area

Most towing companies operate in a well-defined service area. "For most light-duty companies it's about a 25-mile radius from the shop," said Dennis Wencel, author of *The Black Book of Towing*. By contrast, heavy-duty towing companies usually operate within a radius of 50 to 125 miles depending on market conditions in that area (rural, suburban, urban, traffic issues, competition, and the like).

"The most effective marketing tools are ones that can be targeted specifically to these locations," said Wencel. Advertising that covers a large area (TV and radio, for example) may be more than you need. Conversely, if your advertising tools are too small (door hangers, for example), you may not be reaching far enough for new customers.

The bottom line? take care to tailor your advertising efforts to your specific geographic area, and pay close attention to what your customers want and need when they're looking for a tow.

Safety and Signals: Protecting Your Customers

Casey Burrows of Burrows Wrecker in Pendleton, Ky., related a memorable story about his grandfather, who was also a tower:

> Years ago my grandfather was signaled to "pull-around" at a nearby weigh station. He had failed to attach his tow lights on the towed vehicle.
>
> The DOT officer in no uncertain terms informed my grandfather that he would not leave until the tow lights were on that truck. His words were, "Five feet or five hundred miles, you have got to have tow lights!"

"As simple as it may sound," said Burrows, "we still practice that crotchety old officer's requirement."

That requirement may have saved some lives along the way.

The roadside can be a dangerous place to be, especially for tow truck operators. Angela Roper, former tower and current owner of Nationwide Safety Consulting, said that by the third week of 2012 the towing industry had tallied five line-of-duty deaths and four near misses. "Considering our average in the towing industry is 60 to 70 per year, the odds are not in our favor at this point," said Roper.

Roper asked a critical question of owners, towers and office personnel: "What are you going to do to help control these numbers in your company this year?"

According to Terry Humelsine, senior lead instructor at Wreckmaster, "The safest operator is one who has had the training, gained the knowledge, learned the skills and has a thorough understanding of the importance of using each of them wisely every day."

Connecting with the customer

Upon arriving on scene, the operator's first order of business is, of course, to meet the customer. "Like most towers, looking out for the well-being of the operator of the disabled vehicle is a high priority of ours," said Burrows. "It has even been said that their safety is ultimately our responsibility." Because of this, Burrows continued, the task of protecting the lady or gentleman — who is standing in the travel lanes beside their driver's door when the tow truck arrives — can be quite challenging.

Positioning the tow vehicle is incredibly important, said Humelsine. "You may wish to consider parking the service provider's truck behind the disabled vehicle at a five- to eight-degree angle similar to law enforcement," he explained. "In this way the service provider's vehicle is being used as a 'blocker' to give at most, only a very limited amount of protection."

When meeting the customer, Burrows approaches from the curbside of his vehicle and asks the customer to join him in a safe area. "This is where I introduce myself and ensure that I have all of the information needed to perform my duties," explained Burrows. "I will always suggest that [the customer] take refuge in my warm (or cool) tow truck cab and watch through my rearview camera as I work on their vehicle."

Sometimes the customer is receptive to Burrows' recommendations.

However, if the customer says no, Burrows insists that the customer stay on the curbside of his or her vehicle. "If they choose not to wait, seat-belted, in my truck," said Burrows, "I prefer that they remain behind the guardrail or barrier."

Signs, signals and knowledge

To keep the towing or recovery operation moving along smoothly, operators can take advantage of a variety of safety and signaling devices.

Jack Sullivan, director of training at the Emergency Responder Safety Institute in Richmond, Va., lists some of the basic safety equipment: emergency warning lights, road cones (28" to 36" high, orange with reflective bands), warning signs (48"x 48" preferably), flares (where their use is permitted), high-visibility personal protective equipment for each worker (ANSI compliant vest, jacket or coveralls), and reflective markings on the rear and sides of the tow truck.

Operators should place warning signs ahead of the work area to warn approaching motorists, said Sullivan. In addition, "cones and flares should then be used in a taper fashion behind the work area to move approaching vehicles away from the tow truck and work area," he said.

"Drivers should be wearing high-visibility gear at all times while working near moving traffic," said Sullivan. If work conditions require additional protection, operators should request police assistance or a safety service patrol.

Humelsine added an important note: Operators need to be armed with safety *knowledge* in addition to the proper safety *equipment*. "Many operators simply do not know what many may consider as minimal information for towing," explained Humelsine. This information includes legal axle weights, gross vehicle weight and/or gross combination weight limits, length, width and height limits.

Safer controls and brakes

At Burrows Wrecker, all of the towing vehicles are equipped with controls that allow the operator to do his or her job without stepping to the left side of the vehicle. "As designed by the manufacturer, the standard location of the manual controls is on the *left* side," said Burrows. "On our latest units, we stipulated that the manual controls must be placed on the *right* side." Therefore, if the electronic system fails, the operator isn't exposed to the traffic side of the vehicle.

Burrows likes to tinker with his vehicles to boost their safety characteristics. One of his interests is the braking system. For several years Burrows has been "tapping into" the braking system of the disabled air brake equipped vehicle in order to operate its service brakes from the wrecker.

"I have assembled a few air fittings and short hoses in order to make this process easier," said Burrows. On most vehicles, he noted, fewer than five additional minutes are required to enable the brake system. "We are gradually implementing this process with all of our operators," said Burrows.

Burrows added that this procedure decreases stopping distance and makes for a safer towing combination.

Lighting it up

Another of Burrows' special modifications involves the light bar. "I have wired one of our tow light bars so that when an extra wire in the light cord is energized an LED strobe in the bar will flash a quad flash pattern," said Burrows. By triggering this special flash pattern early in the hookup process, the operator ensures that oncoming drivers take notice of what's happening on the shoulder.

The use of lights as roadside warning devices "is permissible and recommended in most areas throughout North America," noted Humelsine. "However, the use of rotating or flashing lights alone is insufficient when performing a roadside service."

Humelsine recommends that the operator use additional warning devices. Towers looking for more information can check out the drivers' Federal Motor Carrier Safety Regulations (FMCSR) handbook and the Manual on Uniform Traffic Control Devices (MUTCD) handbook.

All lights on the carrier and truck should be in proper working order at all times, noted Humelsine. "Information on the legal and proper use of those lights, especially those rotating and/or flashing lights, can be obtained from your municipal, county, state or provincial law enforcement agency."

Additional information related to lighting, its candlepower and its proper use may be obtained from your state's department of transportation, continued Humelsine. That information will include the permissible color and any optional colors for the use of those rotating and or flashing lights, when they are to be displayed and when they are forbidden.

Lights of the future: LEDs

Sullivan points to LED-driven emergency lighting products as a good example of rapidly developing technology that improves safety for towers.

However, Sullivan noted that LED lights also have their drawbacks. "We›re hearing complaints from drivers about glare from the new light bars," he said, "especially at night." Operators should be familiar with their safety light bars and make use of high power/low power switches, explained Sullivan. "The low-power setting should be used at night, to reduce the glare from the emergency lights that often prevents approaching drivers from being able to see operators working near their trucks or the disabled vehicle."

Sullivan said that one available product — the Federal Smart Siren Control Panel — features a low-power button on the bottom left of the device. Other light bar control devices have a similar setting.

Sullivan also cautioned operators to make sure their rear-facing work lights don't blind oncoming drivers. "This is especially evident with flatbeds and rollbacks, when their rear platform is raised," said Sullivan. "Often the work lights are shining right at oncoming drivers, and late at night this can cause the drivers to lose their night vision." As a result, oncoming drivers can't see the tow operators on the side of the road.

The remedy? Operators should tilt the work lights down, said Sullivan, so the lights shine on the work area and not just point backward at oncoming drivers.

Safety planning

"Do you have a 2012 Safety Plan for your business?" asked Roper. Creating a written plan forces you to consider all of your requirements and options when protecting your operators and customers from harm.

Roper outlined some of the critical elements of a safety plan: First, she noted that towers need to update their employee policies to include information from safety meetings, drug policies, CSA (Comprehensive Safety Analysis) 2010, and training, among other things.

"How about all of your equipment?" continued Roper. "Have you given it a good look? Now, I know you might say the drivers do pre-trips and it would be covered in there... Really? Maybe it's time to go truck to truck, clean out the tool boxes and see just what lives in there!

Often in our busy everyday towing, we check off our pre-trip and don't really check out everything on our trucks."

Paperwork can be a good thing

If you hate paperwork, look at it as something that helps maintain good safety in the workplace. "Safety isn't just to be learned in trainings we attend or seminars," said Roper. "It needs to start in the office." She explained that paperwork is "the best way to protect you and everyone else. Make sure your policies cover everything: trucks, equipment, pre-trips and meetings."

Roper has appeared as an expert witness in several court cases where, she said, "paperwork saved the company."

"Covering your 'hiney' is always a good practice, as many of you know," said Roper. "The practice starts with paperwork and ends with the drivers. It is their 'hiney' on the line every day out there." Roper said that these guidelines apply even to companies that have only two tow trucks and tow a hundred cars a year.

Good policies and procedures are the basis for a safe business, said Roper, and follow-up is the key. Attaboys such as driver incentives and safety awards are a great way to increase productivity and morale among your employees, she said.

"I've heard it said many times that 'knowledge is power,'" said Humelsine. "That much is true. However, it is most true only if it is safely and wisely used."

Jack Sullivan's Top 5 Tips on Doing the Job Safely

Jack Sullivan, director of training at the Emergency Responder Safety Institute in Richmond, Va.:

1. Awareness and operations safety training for all tow operators on at least an annual basis.

2. Daily inspections of tow vehicle and safety equipment, including all emergency and warning devices and personal protective gear.

3. All operators should wear high-visibility PPE (personal protective equipment) whenever and wherever they are exposed to moving traffic.

4. Deploy temporary traffic control devices (signs, cones, flares, etc.) as appropriate and available for each work area.

5. If additional scene safety is needed, request assistance from the appropriate resource (law enforcement, DOT, another tow operator, etc.).

Safety tips from Terry Humelsine

Advice from Terry Humelsine, senior lead instructor at Wreckmaster, to operators and owners of towing companies:

- *First*, if you are not a current member, join and support your state's towing association.

- *Second*, encourage and/or support your state association's efforts to have your state government adopt a move-over law that includes tow trucks as well as classifying tow trucks and carriers as emergency vehicles.

- *Third*, encourage your association to provide monthly or bi-monthly seminars with guest speakers representing various government agencies on subjects such as, does your state recognize carriers and/or tow trucks as emergency vehicles? If not, why not and how can we have them included?

191

Casey Burrows' Top Three Safety Tips

From Casey Burrows of Burrows Wrecker Service, Inc., in Pendleton, Ky.:

See and Be Seen. Continually observe with all of your senses. Always use reflective and high visibility clothing on the roadside. Always use your tow lights.

Operate under the W.L.L.(Working Load Limit) of Your Equipment. Our equipment is rated for a reason. Some of the ratings you must determine for yourself. An example: Safe towing capacity = ½ Front Axle Weight x Wheel Base) / Overhang.

Don't Let Your Routine Become Routine. Just because you can do the most common jobs in your sleep doesn't mean that you won't forget something. Always complete a mental checklist of important safety items. Don't breeze through daily and monthly equipment and vehicle safety inspections.

Flashlights in the Dark

Another useful tool, said Casey Burrows of Burrows Wrecker in Pendleton, Ky., is the Streamlight Vulcan Flashlight. All of Burrows' vehicles are equipped with this item. "[It] can be operated in a flashing mode that, when placed at the rear of a disabled vehicle, serves to warn oncoming traffic," explained Burrows.

Burrows noted that the use of the Streamlight's flashing mode provides a much better result than the amber beacon lights on the towing vehicles.

"Each of our tow trucks carries two of these lights," Burrows continued. One Streamlight is used by the operator to illuminate his work area; the other flashlight is used to signal oncoming traffic.

It's important to play it safe with such a bright beam of light. "We use caution when positioning the light so the beam is directed slightly away from the oncoming motorists," said Burrows. "Blinding a driver and causing a crash would defeat the intended purpose!"

About the Author

Allan T. Duffin is a freelance writer and television/multimedia producer. He writes books and Internet, magazine, and newspaper articles. For television he has written, produced, co-produced, and developed programs for the History and Discovery networks. Allan is a veteran of the U.S. Air Force. Visit his website at www.aduffin.com.

Books by Allan T. Duffin, available at Amazon.com

Catch the Sky: The Adventures and Misadventures of a Police Helicopter Pilot
Duffin Creative

History in Blue: 160 Years of Women Police, Sheriffs, Detectives, and State Troopers
Kaplan Publishing/Simon & Schuster

The "12 O'Clock High" Logbook: The Unofficial History of the Novel, Motion Picture, and Television Series
BearManor Media

Tow Truck Kings: Secrets of the Towing & Recovery Business
Available from Amazon.com

Tow Truck Kings 2: More Secrets of the Towing & Recovery Business
Available from Amazon.com

TheatreBook: A Compact Guide to Running Your Theatre
Available from Amazon.com

www.ingramcontent.com/pod-product-compliance
Lightning Source LLC
LaVergne TN
LVHW051515080426
835509LV00017B/2065